NO ONE EVER TOLD ME

Questions That Need Answers

BETTY COBLE LAWTHER

Copyright ©2009—Betty Coble Lawther
All rights reserved
ISBN 0-9665115-4-9

MinMar Press
P.O. Box 1658, Brea, CA 92822

Scriptures taken from the NEW AMERICAN STANDARD BIBLE®
Unless otherwise stated
© Copyright The Lockman Foundation 1960, 1962, 1963, 1968, 1971, 1972, 1973, 1975, 1977. Used by permission.

Scripture quotations marked NLT are taken from Holy Bible, NLT copyright © 1996, 2004, 2007 by Tyndale House Foundation used by permission of Tyndale House Publishers, Inc. Carol Stream, IL 60188

New International Version Scripture taken from the HOLY BIBLE, New International Version® NIV® copyright © 1973, 1978, 1984 by International Bible Society. Used by permission of Zondervan. All rights reserved

Scripture taken from The Message copyright © 1993, 1994, 1995, 1996, 20000, 2001, 2002 used by permission of Nav Press Publishing Group

Book design by Rebecca MacKenzie

Printed in the United States of America

CONTENTS

INTRODUCTION
How to discover the real me — 1

1. HOW I GOT HERE
What does your family look like to you? — 8
Siblings or those other people in your house — 16

2. INFLUENCES
Church and God — 19
How friends and peers affect how you see yourself — 26
How have your teachers influenced you? — 28
The opposite sex — 30

3. CULTURE
Are you letting the media be your guide? — 35
Internet—to build you up or make you feel bad about yourself? — 37
Trauma — 39

4. DISCOVERING THE REAL ME
How do I discover the real me? — 41
Defining important labels you wear — 47
How to decide which way is right for me — 51

5. WHAT DOES GOD WANT FROM ME?
What God wants from me — 59

6. LET GOD SPEAK FOR HIMSELF
What makes a secure identity?   67
What God's will is for me   71
What my inheritance is   72

7. GUARANTEED SECURITY
Where does security come from?   79
How to connect with God   81
What my relationship to Christ provides for me   87

8. HOW THIS WORKS FOR ME
What being in Control means   93
How to make what God says work   100
What control looks like in scripture   107

9. REINFORCING MY VALUE
How to reinforce the value God places on me   111

10. COMMUNICATING ME
How to relate who I am in a healthy way   119

11. WHERE DOES ANGER FIT?
The expression of anger is healthy   129

12. LOVE, WHAT IS IT?
How to receive love   137

13. WHY DATE?
What dating has to do with love   143

14. YOUR FUTURE
What are your dreams for the future?   155

ACKNOWLEDGEMENTS

My special thanks...

To the following people who helped me to see the need and begin to form the study that became a book. These are girls and women who are interested in growing and helping young women become more aware of who they are in Christ and how that affects all other relationships.

Laura and Julie Brooks are my precious granddaughters. We have spent many hours discussing these questions.

DeAnna and Erin Swetland are a mother daughter team that are encouragers of one another.

Lauren and Linda Bishop are daughter and mother exploring and sharing God's Word.

Alyssa Allinson a young woman who is pursuing her dreams in films.

My thanks also to the groups of high school girls who were in the pilot program as this material was being developed.

Jenell MacDonald, my daughter, for the hours of editing.

Rebecca MacKenzie for the artwork and setup.

To all the special people in my life that encourage me from day to day.

Dear Reader,

My heartfelt desire for you as you read this book is that you can discover how very valuable you are to Christ as an individual. As this begins to happen you will have a much easier journey through what surrounds you each day in the form of criticism and deception.

Knowing the truth about your relationship to God makes your decisions better for you. There will be less regrets of having missed the abundant life.

Read slowly and make your goal to understand who God is. You are not ready to apply a principle until you can comprehend how it is possible for you to be so special to anyone, especially God. This is not a time to be searching for what you need to be DOING but a time to explore your value in God's eyes.

This trip can change your life in relationship to those around you after it has changed your life. Prepare to think your way through the material.

Betty Coble Lawther

Betty Coble Lawther

💣 *WARNING: If you are guiding others through this study please be sure you have worked though the material for yourself remembering we cannot lead others where we have not gone ourselves.*

Introduction

Wow!

HOW TO DISCOVER THE REAL ME

Mirror, mirror on the wall who is the prettiest, smartest, most popular, best liked, athletic, has the latest fashions that I need to measure up to today? Does this sound familiar to what runs through your head often as you prepare to step out of your house? Did anyone tell you it is dangerous to let others be in charge of who you are?

The teen years are a time for seeking, developing and establishing your identity. If you let society and your peer group define who you are you will be making poor choices in relationships throughout your life.

Who you measure yourself by determines your value for that period of time. Are you interested in a "look alike" kind of life or do you want to explore your own uniqueness?

Who wouldn't like to be able to be secure in who they are and know their value in relationship to others? It is possible for you if you look in the right place. There are many suggestions as to where your value can be found. Explore for yourself to see what is offered.

LOOK AT WHO YOU ARE TODAY

You can be told over and over you are a princess, a daughter of the King, but they are only words unless you understand why you are referred to in that way. This book will help you become personally related to God and others.

You will be living with yourself for all of eternity. It is great if you like who you are but not so great if you are trying to be someone else.

Now is the time for you to learn where your value comes from and how to understand how personal it is. It is a decision only you can make.

You learn by living in today because you cannot change yesterday and you do not know what tomorrow holds. Today is a very precious gift. It is today that you decide which road you will take. I am not talking about deciding what you are going to do as a career but whether or not you choose a full and meaningful life or an ordinary life.

Christ's promise of abundant life requires that you invest yourself in the relationships you desire to have. It happens when you learn who God is for yourself. Fear goes away when you understand that God is for you and only wants good for you.

The following is not a to-do list. The point of this exercise is to let you look at where you are today. It is not a measure saying that you need to change. This just tells you where you are and what you depend on to say you are valuable. You will always begin from where you are.

Rate these statements	True	False
I am valued by God just the way I am		
To be a better Christian, I must try to do everything He wants		
I am not doing enough to have a good relationship with Christ		
I think sometimes that if I were prettier, people would like me more		
I usually don't like who I am		

What are the "names" I call myself?

I feel very good about my relationship with my friends		
I compare myself to others		
I look for what God wants me to do when I read His Word		
I feel good about my relationship with my parents		
I feel very good about my relationship with God		
I am happy with who I am		
I am proud of the choices I have made		
I often think I need a boyfriend to feel loved and accepted		
I do things I know are not right to order to fit in		
I feel like God expects more from me than what I give		

After checking this chart it should help you to see where to begin by looking at who you are and what your belief system is based on today. The decision is where do you want to go from here? What did you observe about yourself? Did you see conflict in your answers?

It is necessary to define what you are looking for. Who is your model for who you want to be? It is easy to follow the trends and do what everyone else is doing. It takes very little thought to follow the crowd. Without even realizing it you follow the crowd.

There is tremendous pressure by the world to get you to conform. This immediately puts you in comparison with others to see if you are okay.

CHOOSE YOUR FOUNDATION

You choose what foundation you will build your life on. Do you want to build on sand or rock?

These words I speak to you are not incidental additions to your life, homeowner improvements to your standard of living. They are foundational words, words to build a life on. If you work these words into your life, you are like a smart carpenter who built his house on solid rock. Rain poured down, the river flooded, a tornado hit—but nothing moved that house. It was fixed to the rock.

But if you just use my words in Bible studies and don't work them into your life, you are like a stupid carpenter who built his house on the sandy beach. When a storm rolled in and the waves came up, it collapsed like a house of cards.[1]

This scripture has become more vivid with the 2005 Tsunami and Hurricane Katrina. We can see the devastation when a foundation is not on solid ground or in a safe place.

It is one thing to hear God's Word and another thing to believe it is for you. God has given you the opportunity to choose what you want to act on.

God's Word is readily available and it is a privilege to know what He says. Hearing and acting on it is not the same thing. You can know a lot of facts yet do nothing with them to benefit your life. After discovering the facts you must understand what they are saying to you. Once you take them into your belief system you will be ready to apply them to your life.

IT IS YOUR DECISION

Your decisions determine what direction you will take in your life. You get to choose what you want to do with your life.

---

1 *Matt. 7:24–27 Message*

God offers a path to a meaningful life but it is yours to choose to walk that way. Many people and events have influenced your thinking to this point.

Would you like to be in charge of the direction you take with God on your side?

Let's look at what you have gathered to work with.

NOTES

HOW TO DECIDE WHAT IS RIGHT FOR ME

Life is similar to a merry-go-round. When you are young someone puts you on the pony and operates the ride. It is usually slow, with an up and down motion, and you hold on tight. You have no control of how fast or slow it goes. As you get older you want the pony to go faster because it is more exciting. This is real to you. This is how you experienced your world—someone else at the controls.

Look at your history to discover how you have come to believe what you believe about life. The first twelve years of life set the norm for you. The model your family provided probably seems right for you even if you did not like it. The way problems were solved was learned in the home growing up. As a child, if you were seen as a person and communicated with, even though you were small, you expected the whole world to be like that. Your world was that way so why doesn't everyone do it that way? You may not be able to understand why others yell, scream, hit, and verbally abuse others to try to get their point heard if you did not experience that kind of behavior.

If the silent treatment was learned as the way to handle difficulties in your home then going to your room and cutting the other person out of your life seems like the right say to handle the situation to you. Avoidance of conflict is normal to you. It is often viewed as "keeping the peace" and the honorable thing to do. Another way to say it is, "Don't make waves, be nice." Many times "nice" is the goal even though it is false because it is saying what the other person wants to hear so there will be no disagreement. It is an easy way to lose your voice.

Scripture calls for "making peace" not keeping peace. *Blessed are the peacemakers, for they shall be called sons of God*[2] which means you need to get involved with the other person and settle your differences. Speak the truth in love. *But speaking the truth in love, we are to grow up in all aspects into Him who is the head, even Christ.*[3]

This verse is saying **BE truth. How do you do that?**

NOTES

You do not have to be unkind when you tell the truth. The truth you share concerns you. It is not about the other person. It is your perspective you are talking about. It is not how you feel about what they should be doing or how they can make you feel better. It is being truthful about your self. This is a distinction you must learn in your communication. This will be explained more fully later in the study.

What has been normal to you in relationships to others up to this time?

NOTES

If it has been building to the relationship then continue on in your growth. If where you are is not encouraging you and building you up, read on for more information.

To this point everyone around you has been pouring into you who they are and how they feel out of their own experiences. This works well up to a point. Now it is time to sort through what has been given you to find the real you. This a lifetime journey and the sooner you begin the more enjoyable your life will be.

2 *Matt. 5:9 NASU*
3 *Eph. 4:15 NASU*

1

HOW I GOT HERE

Parents are the operators of your merry-go-round. You may have heard that you are here because God wanted you here. Others would say you are here to relate to God and to do His will. I would say you are here because a man and a woman chose to be sexually intimate. Your mother and your father chose to use God's plan of procreation and you are the result of that union.

God gave the assignment in the Garden of Eden to a husband and a wife to make babies and populate the earth.

> *God created man in His own image, in the image of God He created him; male and female He created them. God blessed them; and God said to them, "Be fruitful and multiply, and fill the earth, and subdue it; and rule over the fish of the sea and over the birds of the sky and over every living thing that moves on the earth.*[4]

The design of how babies are made is God's. The husband and wife were to carry out the instructions to multiply and fill the earth and rule over it. You are here by the choices made by your parents. They furnished the material that you will be working with to grow your own life. Each person has her own DNA. No one gets perfect material to work with. All of us were given material that has flaws. Sin has injured everyone. No one gets a perfect beginning. I will agree that

[4] *Gen. 1:27–28 NASB*

some seem to get more than others but we all have material with which to work.

Parents are given strict instructions to teach, train, and love their children. This is to be done with God's Word as a guide. *Fathers, do not provoke your children to anger, but bring them up in the discipline and instruction of the Lord.*[5] One of the things that makes us most angry is when we feel that we cannot be heard. It is your responsible to keep the communication lines open from your side.

WHAT DOES YOUR FAMILY LOOK LIKE TO YOU?

The variety of family structures can vary from a Mother and Father, a single parent home, or parents in second or subsequent marriages where there is extended family that consists of siblings that are step, half and natural. Some families skip back a generation and grandparents provide the family. Sometimes you have two families. Or you may have an adopted family or have spent much of your youth in group of foster homes. The important part is not to make a judgment on the family pattern but to recognize what you are working with so you can have the security and encouragement you need to grow.

FITTING IN

Were you a happy child, a sad child, a lonely child, or a child always in the middle of a group participating? Did you see yourself as a valuable part of the family or on the outside looking in?

> Security as a child is provided when you feel included in all that is going on. The lack of family harmony makes the question "How do I fit in?" even more significant. As a child you probably thought, "What part of this conflict is mine? Did I

5 *Eph. 6:4 NASB*

cause it?" There is a need to feel wanted and secure in your home and with your friends.

How is it possible when there is so much disagreement around you? This is where you need to seek answers from the people with whom you have the disagreement. You are not responsible for your family, only for yourself. Learn what you can contribute.

Is there a person that encourages you? Who is that person? Are they still in your life?

Is it possible for you to talk with them? If so, seek them out and seek their counsel to help you decide where you should be working on your own identity.

What do you do when your parents argue? What does this have to do with you?

I can remember at age twelve counseling my parents. I could not stand the feeling of tension between them. I asked my father to tell me what was happening. He told me what he thought the problem was. I immediately told him how I saw the situation and he apologized to my mother. He had been given wrong information by my grandmother. It was not my responsibility to work on my parent's marriage. Because of the relationship I had with my parents I could ask a hard question and get an answer. Sometimes a child worries and does not know why they feel insecure. It is always best to ask and find out. If you cannot talk with your parent find an adult you respect and let them help you seek the course you should be taking.

If you are not living with both parents what does that say about you?

> Nothing, except that you have more traveling back and forth to do. You are not a part of the marriage. It is not about you. It is about your mother and father being able to work together. Marriage is the parent's assignment. You are only responsible FOR you. You only get one person, yourself, to work on in your whole life. The sooner you begin to practice this the happier you will be. It also gives you plenty of time to do the things you want to do to grow.

Has anyone told you God's assignment for you?

> God does not hold you responsible FOR another person, only FOR yourself. If you could be responsible FOR others you would desire that every person come to know Christ but that is a personal decision that each person must make. You only get one person, yourself, to work on in your whole life. God is the only one who really knows who you are and He desires that you come to know how much help He has for you to learn how valuable a person you are.
>
> If you are trying to live someone else's life so you will be comfortable, you will fail. It is impossible to control another person. You can manipulate them but not for long. Think of how much time and energy you have spent trying to get others to understand you and like you. They may change momentarily but it will not last. Their change will be to try to make you happy or to get you to do something for them.

PARENT'S HOMEWORK

Parents have a God given right and responsibility to instruct their children. *"Children, obey your parents, in the Lord, for this is right."*[6] The child is told to obey her parents. This means you are to listen and pay attention to what they are instructing you to do because they are trying to help you. When you are belligerent and resist what they are saying you are being disrespectful. The instruction to obey is to help you learn. You may not agree but you do not have the experience to make a judgment of your parent's teaching.

You are growing out of the merry-go-round and ready to try the roller coaster. This ride goes faster and has more up and down motions and is much more thrilling. You are still not the operator. While you are no longer a little child you are not an adult either. Let's call this the (parenthesis stage) of your life. It is time to take responsibility for being a part of the family. Obedience teaches you how to learn from others who care about you. It is time for you to get more involved in your training. There is much more to be learned when you decide to be a part of the interaction.

Parents need to hear and see you involved in the learning pattern. If you do not understand what they are asking of you ask for more information. If you do not agree with what is being said it is time for you to share more about where you are in relationship to the subject. Parents need to have current information from you and they can only receive what they need to help them guide you if you are willing to talk with them.

Not all instruction is going to be right because there are no parents that know exactly what needs to be taught in every situation. Be patient and participate. They need information that you have.

It is from the influence and the training you receive in your family that you learn to form your own convictions. What you

6 Eph. 6:1 NASU

believe about yourself, God and others ultimately will be your choice. Take advantage of the learning time with your parents by listening well and seeking to understand what is being said and why. The time will come when you will say, "Stop the roller coaster! I want to get off and choose my own ride through life."

How hard it is to tell the truth? Do you know how important truth is?

> Tell the truth and win your parent's trust. It is only hard when you are more interested in doing what you want than being honest and building trust. It is up to you to become trustworthy before parents can trust you. It is hard to tell the truth when you know what you say is not going to be received or accepted. Give them honest information anyway. In order to do this you must want the relationship with them more than you want their approval.

Deceit is common and the easy way out but it destroys a relationship because it destroys trust. Parents want the best for you. Information is needed from you about you to establish trust.

Parents are fearful for your physical safety because they know some of the mistakes you can make will have lifetime consequences. They are fearful for your mental health because if you are given the wrong information you may be easily convinced or deceived. They are fearful for you emotionally that you may be injured in relationships with friends and peers by letting your feelings be your guide.

Some parents are fearful you will receive incorrect teaching or poor role models. This may cause them to hover over you and ask far too many questions to suit you.

When parents have a difficult time trusting you it may

come from their own backgrounds where they have been disappointed. **Talk with them about where they were and the decisions they had to make when they were your age.**

Conflicts with parents CAN BE RESOLVED.

It is easy to think parents don't understand, but take into account they have a larger view of life than you do. Many times they are trying to protect you from the pitfalls they have encountered in their lives. Many teens want to experience life themselves and aren't concerned what the consequences might be. It is easy to think what you want to do is innocent but you have little experience to know where it will lead. Or you may think you can get by with what you are doing and nothing bad will happen to you.

Keeping secrets gives you the illusion you can do what you want to do without any consequences. You may feel you have control or the upper hand in the situation. Instead secrets put you in bondage. The truth will eventually come to light.

I am not assuming that parents are always right. Parents are not perfect but they have the assignment when they bring you into the world to teach, train, and to love you the very best they know. A mom who has not discovered her valued identity may be critical and living out of her own frustration with herself. Ask her about her childhood. This could give you a better understanding of her.

There is a time in this stage of your life when you want to be on your own and being with your parents is embarrassing to you. When this happens talk with your parents and explain to them how you are feeling and thinking so they will not feel you are just being difficult. If they enjoy being with you they may not be able to understand why you do not have the same need as they do.

What is wrong with listening to what your parents say and learning from it?

> It is a good time for you to ask questions about things that concern you. Do not let it be a one way conversation. Participate. Gathering information gives you much more to work with in building the relationship.

Somewhere in early life the message begins to be communicated that your value and love only come when everything is done right and everyone agrees. In Christian homes it should be understood that God values everyone. Unfortunately, the words are said but are not acted out in the relationships. You may not even hear the message of God's love for you because you are criticized often by a parent for not reaching a certain level of achievement. It is easy to feel a sense of value when you do things that are pleasing to your parents. When perfection is not reached then failure is assumed. You need to rethink this and ask yourself if you are striving for perfection to be valuable or are you listening to God say how valuable you are to Him? Performing to be valuable will always fail in the end because you cannot be perfect.

From time to time you have probably been ready to trade your parents in for new ones or maybe ones that would be more cooperative; ones you could talk with and would not be pushing you to always learn a lesson. Parents are here to help guide you into adulthood. Think about how much you listen to them and value what they say to you. Adults are hard to understand, but let's try. They have information to give you that can be of help in making decisions for your life.

Your parents are nervous for fear they will not teach you and protect you from all harm. Parents may put pressure on you to make up for what they think you have not learned because of your behavior. That is why it is so important for you to communicate with them. I hear you say, "But they don't listen." Your responsibility is to tell, not to make them listen.

Could it be that you are "using" your parents to get what you want rather than to learn?

Are you telling only the part of the story that you think they will agree with? Do not give up telling them where you are and how you feel about your life. They are listening more than you think. They may not know what to do with the information you are giving them. Keep talking.

Do you "bad mouth" your parents to look cool or independent?

If you do it only makes you look immature and it does not help the relationship. Later in the book we will discuss this more.

Often parents will move into the "fix it mode" to find a quick solution. Listen. Be patient. It is only time for you to speak when you have listened to what they have said. It is best not to argue with them but to ask questions about the decision and then tell them how that makes you feel.

Parents are to be representatives for God in guiding you when you are young. They are not the same as God. They are to teach you who God is and how to follow Him by their example and instruction. Since everything in life is imperfect you will not find perfection in this life. Their success and failure to paint an accurate picture of God has brought you to your belief about God. It is time for you to know God by His Word, the Bible, and not what others say about Him.

It is difficult to understand that God values you where you are today if your parents never seem to be pleased with what you do. God does not require that you change for Him to value you. He is willing to work with you where you are in the circumstances you are in today. He only works with you in the present anyway so it would be useless for Him to ask you to do something or be someone in your tomorrow. Who you are is what you are becoming.

> *Give your entire attention to what God is doing right now, and don't get worked up about what may or may not happen tomorrow. God will help you deal with whatever bad things come up when the time comes.*[7]

It is not the "becoming" but the "being" that builds your relationship with God. This is contrary to the "World System" and ideas of relationships. The world completely leaves God out as a relational person. He is portrayed as a harsh disciplinarian who is out to get you. This is what confuses your identity and value. Now is the time for you to know God by His word, the Bible, and not what others say about Him.

HOW DO YOU DEFINE YOU?

Life is confusing for both you and your parents. There are so many choices. One choice is to get to know your parents as individual people and let them get to know you as you change and grow. Another choice is to assume who your parents are and let them guess who you are. Which of these choices lead to understanding each other?

This section of the book will look at the people that have influenced how you see yourself as a person. Look carefully at how much of what you believe about yourself comes from the people part of your world.

SIBLINGS OR THOSE OTHER PEOPLE IN YOUR HOUSE

Some of your belief system has been formed by your position in the family. There is also the false concept of what a family should look like. It is easy to look at others and feel they

---

[7] Matt. 6:33–34 *The Message*

have it all together and everyone loves everyone and they get along well. It looks like everyone is best friends and they like all of the same things; however, families are made up of unique individuals. People disagree with one another. We do not all enjoy doing the same things. The challenge is to grow healthy relationships where you are by allowing each person to be who he or she is. You must be yourself.

How do you see your place in the family? Are you an only child, the oldest, middle, youngest, or the one coming into a new situation that is "blending" you in? Stepping into a ready made family may be difficult. It may make you feel smashed into a mold that is unfamiliar. Take time to adjust if you are joining in a new family. Learn how to become acquainted with the new people. While this is a challenging time it is also a time to explore who you are in this particular situation.

There are two huge problems with siblings—comparison and selfishness.

You only have control of how you relate to others. You cannot prevent others comparing you but you can stop comparing yourself with others. You are YOU not someone else. You do not expect an apple and an orange to be alike. You may like one more than the other but you do not expect them to be the same. Look at all of the individual traits and looks you have that are unique.

Take a few minutes and make a list of the positive ways you are an individual in your family. How does your individuality add to the family?

Be a positive part of the family looking for ways to contribute who you are to your siblings, be they natural or step. You have the choice to say who you are. If you become labeled as the "difficult one" it is time for you to communicate how you feel and what you are willing to do to correct the image that

> has been put on you. If this is not who you are it is necessary for you to say who you are because you are the only one who can. Examine your actions and see if you are trying to get the attention of your parents by your misbehaving. If you feel you are not being heard, talk to one of your parents alone and tell them how you are feeling. Do not threaten. Seek a solution.

Selfishness comes from insecurity about how valuable you are in the family. Always wanting your own way is a sure sign you are not interested in others. Learn to give or invest yourself without trying to get something for yourself. If you want to reinforce your worth, follow Jesus' saying,

In everything I did, I showed you that by this kind of hard work we must help the weak, remembering the words the Lord Jesus himself said: 'It is more blessed to give than to receive.[8]

Your opinions and the opinions of others are just that, opinions. Agreement with others should not determine what you value. Learning to value your own opinion is a very good place to develop who you are in relationship with others. Since you are responsible FOR yourself it is healthy to decide what you really value in each situation you encounter.

---

8 *Acts 20:35 NIV*

2

INFLUENCES

CHURCH AND GOD

Your Church and your knowledge of God have formed your belief system about you, others, and God. Let's look at how this has happened.

Children notice everything. They may not have words to describe what is going on but they are affected emotionally and this contributes to their belief about who they are and who God is. It is important for you at this age to realize that Church and God are not one and the same. The people in the church may fail you but God never will. It may seem God is failing you because you do not know who He is and what He says to you. You are to a place in your life where you can begin to study for yourself who God says He is.

Sunday school teachers that make the stories come alive for you may have been interested in making a point of how you are to behave. Perhaps that is the way you understood it. Probably most of what you know about God is from your Sunday School lessons, Bible stories, books you have read and sermons you have heard. All of these sources have contributed to what God is like to you. This book is here to help you grow in your personal knowledge of who God wants to be to you.

There may come a time when it is a battle to attend church and Bible study. **Have you had a time when it has not been**

cool to your friends to go to church so you want to stay at home rather than attend church? Maybe you have been in church all of your life and the stories are old to you. It is time to gain a better understanding so you can find applications later. Lack of understanding of who God is begins to cause confusion within you. Confusion can create a false guilt when you try to live by what others think you should or should not be doing. Or you may feel you are not good enough because you cannot do it all right.

Guilt is appropriate only when you have done something wrong. You will feel guilty if you are a hypocrite, imposter, fake, fraud, counterfeit, pretender. These reactions are caused many times by false information. It is so important for you to understand that **God is who He says He is and that He has done what He says He has done for you. Do you believe this?** If you pretend to believe when you do not understand you will feel empty. This may cause you to think and feel that God does not really care about you. The result is that you live your life as you please without consideration for what God says in His word. The other path you may take is that you just feel guilty. Often the inappropriate behavior of adults will cause you to think that God is not who people have lead you to believe He is. Go to His word and see what He says.

Christ loved the church and gave Himself for it. He set up the church as a group gathering together as believers in Him to support, encourage, and teach one another. It is helpful to see church as part of your family. Meaningful relationships are established in your fellowship together. Make it one of your goals to be a healthy member of the church.

Does your knowledge about God come from looking at Him in a functional way or a relational way? Let's check.

Prayer is a good place to look at how you see God. **Do you pray as if God is the great genie?** I have had young women ask me to pray for them that they would not be pregnant after they had already had intercourse the night before with their boyfriend. Prayer is not a fix-it-all after I have done as I please.

What is prayer anyway but your way of communicating with God about where you are and listening to Him from His Word tell you who He is? Prayer should be about you and God. It is supposed to be a personal relationship. You may pray for everyone around the world and never touch your personal relationship with God.

Prayer is a personal conversation with God about you and Him. When talking with a good friend it is not a problem to find topics of conversation. In fact most teens are accused of always talking with their friends. With the cell phone this is possible 24/7. What do you talk about? Everything.

Why is it so hard to talk to God?

You know He already knows who you are, where you are and what you are concerned about. But you do not have that all worked out in your mind. Talking with Him helps you get answers to what you can do about your situations.

You can only carry on a conversation when the other person is accessible. Since God's Holy Spirit lives in you, if you are a believer, He is always available. You do not have to leave a voice mail or wait in line.

Some of the reasons conversation with God is difficult:
- I seem to be having the conversation with myself.

    He is not talking back—why?

    You must be willing to read the text message. His word to you—the Bible.

- Is most of the conversation what He should be doing to make life easy for you or the people you care about?

- You may have heard someone say God says, "Yes, No,

or Wait" when you prayer to Him. Where is this in Scripture? He always hears you. He even knows what you need before you ask but you need to learn that you must express yourself to Him. The lessons He is offering to teach you are written in His Word. Learn to listen to who He says He is when you are reading the Bible.

- You do not realize that He is on your side. He loves you unconditionally and always wants the best for you. You do not have to perform right for Him to love you. He loves you just the way you are.

What do I talk with Him about? God knows everything about everything. Why do I need to talk with Him? Having knowledge does not create a personal relationship. A relationship calls for interaction. It isn't one sided.

What is God's part? God made a plan before the foundation of the world was created so it would be possible for you to relate to Him if you choose. We will discuss this more later.

What is your part?

A common Christian saying is, "It is not all about You." No, you are not the center of the universe and others are not here to cater to you. However, you are the only one to represent you in your relationship with God or others. It is yours to choose to accept what God says and let Him be your God. After you have chosen Him you begin your part of the relationship. You talk with Him about who He is and who you are. You talk to Him about what is troubling you. What concerns you. How you want to work something out in your life.

HOW TO BECOME CLOSE TO GOD

What makes a relationship personal? Is it when you can connect with each other and share who you are without fear of rejection? Connection comes when you accept Him as your God. He is available to you. The Bible is His way of sharing with you who He is. Are you willing to share who you are without fear of rejection? God is not in the business of rejecting you but of encouraging you and loving you. He is there for you.

What does He say about His relationship to you?

Stay away from the love of money; be satisfied with what you have. For God has said, "I will never fail you. I will never leave you." That is why we can say with confidence, "The Lord is my helper, so I will not be afraid. What can mere mortals do to me!" [9]

What do you want in your relationship with God?
A chatty friend?
One who listens to you?
You learning to listen to Him accurately?
Knowing God is for you?
>NOT the big rule keeper always finding something wrong that needs to be corrected.

Acceptance?
Loyalty?
Encouragement?
Commitment to your well being?
Honesty?

All of this is offered to you if you choose to relate to God.

Do you have a good friend that all you do is ask them to do something for you? If you had a friend that bossed you around like a servant would you be building a good relationship with them? Look at how you relate to God. **Are you always asking Him to do something for you?** Read His word to you looking for who He says He is and what He has provided for you to enjoy.

---

9 *Heb. 13:5–6 NLT*

CONNECTIONS IN THE CHURCH

It is helpful to have a person to relate to whom you admire. They are usually called a mentor and the church is a good place to find one. Look at their relationship with God and others and then ask them if they would be willing to talk with you occasionally or on a regular basis. Maybe you have a small group leader that is already there for you. It needs to be someone you can talk with, who is non judgmental, comfortable; someone you can look up to and that respects your opinions and will care about you as an individual. This is a ***hands on*** personal relationship that gives you encouragement.

Group activities with your church are another way to develop you socially, relationally, spiritually. It is also a place to find community and support. **Have you found this to be true? If not why not?**

HANDLING GOD'S WORD

Conflict often comes when others tell you who you are and what you are supposed to be doing. Often, the admonition is, "Get into God's Word and find His will or His plan for your life." That is very true but you need to know what you are looking for when you study God's word. It is not a magic book that just by reading it you automatically know how to apply it to life. Application comes after you have an understanding of what is being said. When you read you need to know when it was written, to whom it is written, for what purpose, and in what context.

Here is an example of taking scripture out of context. It is harmful to take a verse of scripture out of context and try to apply it to your life without reading the whole passage. In the Psalms David does a praise to God and he talks about the way He watches over you. I have heard people pull out the phrase that God will heal all of their diseases. You ask, "Who is He talking to and what is He talking about?"

> *A psalm of David. Praise the LORD, I tell myself; with my whole heart, I will praise his holy name.*
>
> *Praise the LORD, I tell myself, and never forget the good things he does for me.*
>
> *He forgives all my sins and heals all my diseases.*
>
> *He ransoms me from death and surrounds me with love and tender mercies.*
>
> *He fills my life with good things. My youth is renewed like the eagle's*
>
> *Bless the LORD, O my soul,*
>
> *And all that is within me,*
>
> *bless His holy name.*
>
> *Bless the LORD, O my soul,*
>
> *And forget none of His benefits;*
>
> *Who pardons all your iniquities,*
>
> *Who heals all your diseases;*
>
> *Who redeems your life from the pit,*
>
> *Who crowns you with loving kindness and compassion;*
>
> *Who satisfies your years with good things,*
>
> *So that your youth is renewed like the eagle.*[10]

It is very easy for someone who has cancer to pull this passage out of context and if they are not healed they say God's word is not true. This is how distortion of God comes about. Is the Psalmist not saying that God desires only good for us? You have an internal healing process in your body that was put their originally by God design. When you cut our hand it will bleed

---

10 Psalm 103:1–5 NASU

for a short time and then your blood begins to clot. You do not understand it all but it still happens.

It is interesting to go to scripture and read Bible stories over again now that you have the ability to think abstractly (an ability that develops in the teen years). It is necessary to reread these stories because now you are able to understand things that you could not understand when you were a child. For instance **what do you know about Daniel in the lion's den?** Did you know Daniel was 80 years old and one of the King's top administrators when he was put in the lion's den? Did you think he was a teenager? Read the story again in Daniel 6.

Was Daniel in the furnace with Shaddrach, Meshach and Abed-nego? Daniel 3. Is what you know from the pictures you saw or from what the scripture says? You probably missed a lot when these stories were read or told to you as a child. David was faithful from his youth. Are you surprised at the age of Daniel and how he related to God all of his life? It is very important for you to go back and study for yourself what scripture says. This book offers you an opportunity to begin to study and understand for yourself who God is to you.

HOW FRIENDS AND PEERS AFFECT HOW YOU SEE YOURSELF

Should you call this time in your life "peer pressure" time? Adults do. Look at how much your friends and peers affect your feeling about yourself. Friends from school, church and community become a large part of influence by the time you have reached your teens. There is pressure from without and from within. Friends are a very important part of your life. Learn to evaluate your friends because they know you best. True friends last a lifetime. A person is fortunate if they have two or three close friends. Most people have only one.

Who is a Friend? It is a person who is dear to you, a

companion, acquaintance, comrade, supporter, helper, someone you can trust, one you have confidence in and who listens to you. A friend is one you feel close to and is like a part of the family. What are you saying when you call someone a friend?

Friends should build you up. I would not call a person a friend who tears me down. The friends you choose say how much you value (respect) yourself. By association you become labeled by the friendships you encourage. The axiom, you are known by the friends you keep, is true. Many are introduced to drugs, sex, and alcohol trying to please and fit in with their so called "friends" and peers.

List the characteristics you would like in a friend.

What are you looking for in a friend? The more honest you are with yourself the easier it will be for you to decide what is acceptable and what is unacceptable to you in character traits in a friend.

How do you choose your friends? Are they from the neighborhood, school, your parents friends' children or where?

How do you get out of a so-called friendship that is wrong for you?

You get to decide where you want to spend your time and with whom. It is always best to address the problem rather than ignore it and hope it will go away. Kindly let the person know that you will not be spending time with them in the future because you are setting some priorities that require other emphasis. Don't put yourself in situations where you know there will be temptations. Be honest with yourself or you may get caught up in "people pleasing" which is not the best for you.

There are a number of levels of friendship. Some friends are just acquaintances that you see occasionally. There are other friends that you do certain activities with such as school, church, music, or sports. Then there is that best friendship that every one hopes to develop. If a person wants friends they need to be friendly. A deceitful person is not worthy of being called a friend.

HOW HAVE YOUR TEACHERS INFLUENCED YOU?

Have you had teachers that were encouraging to you? Think of just one that helped you to see possibilities for you that you had not seen before. It is easier to study a subject when the teacher is interested in you and how well you are learning. They help you to develop new ideas. They inspire you to be a better student. My granddaughter, when she was in eighth grade, had a teacher say to her, "Believe in yourself or no one else will." That statement has made a big difference in her search for who she is.

Discouraging remarks rarely motivate learning. They make you feel bad about who you are. They also inflict false guilt. You have not done anything wrong but you feel you are disappointing the teacher. This makes for a gloomy student who finds it difficult to improve. Working from the negative gives you no material with which to work. When you look at what you do right you have something with which to work. Even if your teacher does not see your good qualities it does not keep you from majoring on them so you can be a better learner.

How do you learn best?

Are you a visual learner, a hands on learner, do you do best reading it yourself or do you learn best by hearing? Teachers are a great influence but they are not the ones who say who you are.

Do you like school? If not, why not?

Are you bored? Where does your boredom come from? Is it from monotony, dullness, laziness, slowness, day dreaming, exhaustion, or weariness or are you just not interested in being in charge of your life and your decision to get a good education?

Are you too busy trying to stay in the "know" with your

friends? Always trying to have the latest information about others can turn into "gossip" when it becomes telling all so you can be one up on everyone else. That is not what school is for.

No one likes to think they are wasting their time. **Are most of your teachers understanding of you?** They can only know you if you will interact and communicate with them. Talk with them or write a note asking the questions you have. As in any profession, there are good teachers and bad. There are some with unhealthy personal agendas and others who put the best interest of the student first. You are there to learn the course material so work to understand what is being said.

What is the most difficult part of school for you?

Is it pressure to make good grades?

Are you being compared with others when it comes to your report card?

Is it pressure to decide what you are going to do with the rest of your life?

Is school a safe place for you?

The American Association of University Women released a study, "Hostile Hallways," that documents what girls are experiencing. It reports that 70% of girls experience harassment and 50% experience unwanted sexual touching in their schools. One third of all girls report sexual rumors being spread about them, and one-fourth report being cornered and molested. The study says that the classrooms and hallways of our schools are the most common sites for sexual harassment. Many girls are afraid to speak up for fear of worse harassment.

If you do not feel safe at school I would suggest you find an adult that you trust and talk with them. The school counselor would be a place to begin. Many times nothing is done because girls will not report what is going on.

THE OPPOSITE SEX—YOU OR THE GUYS?

A five year old girl came running to her mother with the question, "Which one of us is the opposite sex?" Since this is a book for girls it has to be the boys.

YOUR APPROVAL RATING

Boy/Girl relationships at this stage of your life are very confusing. Your home, school, and church experiences play a big part in how you see yourself. If you have had only good experiences with your father, brother, and boys who are friends you are probably comfortable around boys. The main awkwardness will come if you are trying to please them to win their attention and approval. In order to be comfortable with boys learn to be yourself whether they approve or not. It is very important that you respect yourself enough to be honest with yourself.

Bad experiences with males may cause you to seek to be in control of the relationship so you will not get hurt again. This is acted out in many different ways such as:

Your attitude may be I will hurt them before they hurt me.

Money. I can go more places if they pay. Using.

Social acceptance—everyone has a boyfriend so to be accepted I will do whatever it takes.

Mean behavior to all males because you believe they are all bad.

I will show them I can be equal by sleeping around and using them. Is this not stooping to a lower level to try to be equal?

Maybe you have been raised in a single parent home by your mother and you do not have brothers so you are not familiar with the behavior of boys. This may cause girls to seek male attention at any price.

Being Accepted—what does it take?

Are you interested in being attractive or seductive?

Are you dressing to look your best or are you trying to attract the attention of every male around you? You may say, "I just want to be *in* and everyone dresses this way." This comes back to trying to be one of the crowd instead of being who you are. How you dress says a lot about you. Be your own person.

Necklines exposing your breasts say you want others to see you as sexy. Does this make you more accepted or more observed? I overheard the comment from a young woman to a young man staring at her breast, which were very exposed, "Here is my face," pointing to her face. His remark was, "I can't see your face for your boobs."

A young woman is charming and attractive when she is being true to herself. Self respect is a very drawing characteristic to have. It means that you are not going against or violating something that is important to you to entice others. You are not trying to find your worth in others but understand your own value as a person.

Your standard for morality says a great deal about how you see yourself. **Are you in charge of who you are or do you let those around you say what you have to do to be acceptable to them?**

What is sexual immorality to you?

This question was answered in a group of teens who said, "Adultery, homosexuality, sex before marriage, and pornography."

What do you use as a standard for morality?

Do you feel a need to be careful so you will not offend anyone? Tolerance is a by-word today meaning anything goes. If you listen to the "world system" there should be no right or wrong, and

> today's standard is do whatever you want to do because you are only young once. It is true that you are only young once but what you do today will affect your future just like what you have done up to this time of your life is affecting you today.

Inappropriate touching is called abuse. Sexual comments are abuse. What is called appropriate is not to be set by the standard of the day but is determined by how much respect you have for yourself. **Are you out there to be used or maybe to use others so you can be included by your peers?**

Is having a boyfriend what determines your self-worth?

Exclusive relationships with one boyfriend limits your being able to experience different personalities and characteristics in friendship. This causes an unhealthy stress on you and can cause you to make unwise decisions on selecting friendships with boys.

Your objective should not be to please boys but to get acquainted with who they are and share who you are. Self-respect is big here. Value yourself enough to walk away if all he is interested in is you pleasing him.

Abandonment and rejection are big fears. If you are making your own decisions and in control of your own life the other person's decision to walk away indicates you will not be controlled by trying to please them. You are in charge of making the decision of what is acceptable to you.

When you become a friend with a guy that wants you to be only with him be careful. This is a sign of an unhealthy relationship. One friendship should not isolate you from other friends. Exclusiveness in friendship is a form of control.

Peer Pressure is often applied in boyfriend relationships by talk about you that may not be true. Sometimes boys make up stories that are not true to make them look "cool." Sometimes girls tell lies because they are jealous of your friendship. Be your own person and do not bend under the pressure of your peers. Be the unique person you are not a "cookie cutter" image.

According to Proverbs 7:4 the best friend to have is wisdom and understanding.

Say to wisdom,"You are my sister,"
And call understanding your intimate friend;

3

CULTURE

ARE YOU LETTING THE MEDIA BE YOUR GUIDE?

Unrealistic models are air brushed and retouched.

What is cool in your group? How much effort do you put forth to call attention to you?

Superficial—who can look perfect? **By whose standard do you want to live?** Every girl has beauty that is hers alone at this particular stage of her life. You may not be able to see it now. Remember that beauty is inside out. Who you are shows on your face.

Eating disorders are an ongoing battle for many young women who use the "World System" as a guide for their life. To satisfy a need for today it may lead to many serious health problems physically and emotionally. Some sober questions are, "**Do you feel food is the only thing you are in control of in your life? Are you trying to make a statement to yourself that you are okay? Are you so lost in who you are that being in control of food is necessary?**" If this has happened to you or you fear it is happening to you get help. Talk to someone you trust. Call a help line and discuss it with the counselor there. Do something now. Do not wait thinking it will correct itself or just go away. You are forming habits that will affect the rest of your life.

TV shows are trying to dictate to you how you must

look, what clothes you must have, how to treat your friends, the attitude you should have and the status you must obtain to have value. The attitude is "anything goes." Being ugly and rude seems to be norm for the day.

Sex—normal and healthy

> Be sure your information is true. Most of what is portrayed is there to eventually steal from you your value as a person. The message that sex is a "game of use" and is not personal is a false message. I will discuss this further later.

Television, the media and DVD's are trying to say to you there is no such thing as morality and immorality. Their message is for you to decide what is right and wrong. My question is **what guideline will you use to determine what is right and wrong for you?** Do you have enough experience to make this determination? Can you make a decision from experience if there is no absolute? You must choose what you are going to use as a guideline for your life. Be thoughtful in your choice because it can determine the tone for the rest of your life.

Take a long look at the lives of the celebrities you admire. Look at their lives and evaluate for yourself. What do they have going for them but being in the public eye all of the time? Sometimes when they are on top of the chart of popularity they have money but if you check on them in later years many of them are bankrupt financially, emotionally and especially relationally.

MAGAZINES

Contradicting message.

Articles saying "Don't have sex…until you are ready. What does that mean? How do you know when you are ready? We will discuss this later when we talk about where you are going with your life.

There are many articles on how to connect, to belong, to be popular, and to have friends. All have the same message: Thin is Beautiful. They say sexual experience is necessary.

MOVIES

Plot—A strong message is given that in order to be happy sex needs to be tried.

Homosexuality is viewed as normal.

Happily ever after the end.

Sex is the way to be loved.

In all of the media TOLERANCE is the big idea. **Tolerance of all behavior says you do not have a standard set for yourself.** You are just going along with what is easy or popular. This is a good way to lose your identity. A quick way to lose control of your life is to tolerate everything and everyone that comes along as if they are telling the truth.

Truth is necessary in order to make healthy decisions.

INTERNET
TO BUILD YOU UP OR TO MAKE YOU FEEL BAD ABOUT YOURSELF?

We live in an electronic world. We communicate constantly through cell phone, texting, email and the internet. Electronic communication can be a playful thing that brings excitement but the internet and other electronic communication can also have long term consequences. Technology lets us be connected on a certain level with friends. It is possible to display an image for another to see. Many girls feel they need a sexy image to be accepted. Putting a picture, of yourself or maybe one of your friends putting a picture of you, on the internet can be harmful. It never will go away. You may be putting yourself out there to be used. Andre Vachss who fights this terrible crime against children says, "The image of a sexually displayed child—be it a photograph, a tape or a DVD—records both the rape of the child and an act against humanity."

Using sexual expressions on the internet will indicate you are an open target to a predator. Establishing a false identity says you do not want a relationship you are just killing time or deceiving others. **Do you think you are safe?** You are not.

Be truthful and be who you are. You don't have to try to impress or seduce. Use the internet for research for information you are studying. It can also be a place for social interaction. Be honest about yourself and exercise self-respect.

A social network such as My Space should not be a measure for valuing yourself by the number of hits or to see how popular you are by the number of "friends" who respond. It is not an indication of how many real friends you have. **What image are you trying to present?**

If there is an empty space in your heart that needs to be filled, take a good look at where you have been looking to fill it. **Have the things you have looked at filled the emptiness or the nothingness you feel? What exactly is it that you are looking for?** Is it to feel loved? To feel safe? To be accepted as you are? To be significant to someone? To feel you belong? OR…To be good enough? To be connected?

You can never be good enough and you may say, "Then why try?" Good question. The person you are trying to please would have to completely control you to meet their needs or wants for you to be accepted all of the time. It just does not happen permanently. Tomorrow they want something else from you. "People pleasing" is not being true to yourself. If you are always trying to be pleasing to others, you can never be developing your true self.

If you are trying to fill the emptiness by comparison of yourself with others you will not succeed for more than a brief time. Since no two of us are alike, it makes comparison useless whether it is grades, accomplishments, looks, or whatever. Measuring by someone else just doesn't work permanently.

How about discovering who you are today and letting her have the freedom to grow and share the young woman God sees as very very valuable? He gives you room to be less than perfect and still be loved.

TRAUMA

Many forms of abuse take place because of the use of drugs and alcohol. The big cover-up of emotional pain with the use of drugs and alcohol takes many forms. It leads to sexual abuse, verbal abuse, abandonment, both physically and emotionally, and many other injuries.

Inappropriate touching, observing, or speaking can say to a little girl that she was not good enough to be accepted and loved. Many times she will think she is bad and caused this to happen to her. She will often get the message that this is normal behavior because an adult is in charge.

When you realize these behaviors are not healthy behaviors, it is time for you to reveal the secret. Keeping this secret will put you in bondage. If you keep the secret it will tie you in knots. It lowers your self-worth because you are accepting responsibility for something that was done to you. It was not something you initiated.

There are other traumas such as: bodily injury, shock, such as an accident or a death, painful emotional experiences such as moving or divorce that can hinder you because you have not had the opportunity to talk them though and heal from them. Talk with someone who has had similar experiences and let them help you express your loss. In addition you may want to consider seeking a professional counselor.

Pornography is rampant in our society. "Every sexual fantasy is an attempt to heal the woundedness in your spirit."[11] Where has that woundedness come from?

According to statistics more and more girls are becoming "school refusers," meaning they do not want to attend school because of what they experience. There is a daily lack of respect in the halls of the schools. There is touching, fondling and sometimes even overt molestation going on. Report this to the school counselor. If you are not heard by the counselor go to a teacher or the school superintendent. You must speak up now because denying it will only make it harder for you later.

What messages are boys picking up that they treat girls like property, an object for their use? Boys and men get the message from the media that girls are just sex objects. Girls may buy into that message also, to their later regrets. You have an obligation to yourself to stand firm in who you are and not allow this kind of behavior toward yourself.

Trauma has many blinding effects on young lives. Be sure when you become aware that something is not right that you seek out someone who knows where you are and can help you work through the trauma. Your life will be more in balance and decisions will be much easier when you are not excusing wrong behavior toward you. Your belief system about you will change. You deserve respect. Require it from those around you as a condition for friendship.

Where does the value to stand up for yourself come from? It comes from receiving the value that God places on you as your own. What has happened to you in the past will not change but what you do about it now can change your life.

---

11 (Laaser, lecture 2008)

4

DISCOVERING THE REAL ME

HOW DO I DISCOVER THE REAL ME?

Where do I look? The real Me vs. the projected Me. **Why do you think being someone else would be better?**

Most young women are searching in many areas to find who they are. **How much do trends affect you in your search for who you are?** Some are seeking all kinds of experience trying to find who they are. Letting others say who you are or learning the hard way is a pricey way to learn. The people who are setting the standard may be miserable with who they are. **Are you looking for excitement or a sense of identity and belonging?** Do you want to find someone who will make you feel good about yourself?

Teens who select a unique style of dress that will attract attention to themselves do so to feel they are being seen. Do they gain identity? Changing your appearance is a cover up for the lack of identity. They have no place they feel they belong so they try to make a pseudo place of belonging.

Take a look at yourself and assess where you seek value:
- Being one of the "in crowd"
- Attention—recognition of you as a person
- Compliments—flattery
- Achievement—to buy value
- Recognition—as a person—accomplishment saying who you are

- Praise—performance as proof of value
- Number of Friends—quality vs quantity
- Material possessions—a measure of worth
- Clothing—looking at the outside—the person you are inside says character
- Acceptance—use of friendships
- Grades to learn or to cover worthless feelings or a sense of failure where you do not excel or a desire to learn

When you look at your belief system and how it has been formed, you begin to realize how much you depend on what others think of you. Identifying who you really are in the midst of all the instructions and opinions of others is confusing.

What is wrong with just being you?

With the billions of people on the earth it is difficult to think of each one as significant. In fact, each one is not significant to everyone, but we are all significant to God. I have met many young women who felt they were not very important to anyone. I want to take you through a journey that will give you the foundation to build confidence in who you are, how important you are, and why you are here.

YOUR VALUED IDENTITY—WHERE DOES IT COME FROM?

It is necessary, in order for you to feel confident, to establish the basis of value that you are working from. Take a look in the mirror. **What is your perception of yourself?** What you feel is a byproduct of what you think about yourself. **How do you look at yourself? Are you critical of yourself?** Do you reject your good qualities? Do you feel you are not included or valued by others? I hope you can look at yourself and know you make a valuable contribution to those around you. The way you choose to think about yourself determines what you have to work with that day.

Don't be your own worse enemy by criticizing yourself.

You can take a lesson about criticism from the Apostle Paul as he confronted the hostile world around him when he spoke the following words,

> *It is a very small thing that I should be examined by you, or by any human court. In fact, I do not even examine myself. For I am conscious of nothing against myself, ... but the one who examines me is the Lord. Therefore do not go on passing judgment before the time, but wait until the Lord comes who will both bring to light the things hidden in the darkness and disclose the motives of hearts; and then each person's praise will come to them from God.* [12]

In studying this passage of Scripture can you see how to let what others think be just that, what they think, and you are not responsible to try to change them? Paul was saying to his critics that their opinions did not influence who he was. He even went so far as to say he did not criticize himself because he was relating to Christ the best he could. He said not to pass judgment before the time because God is the only one who sees your heart. **Isn't it interesting that He is looking at what you do right and not what you do wrong?** That is a rare experience in most of our lives. God will give you praise for choosing to relate to Him.

Stop and think. Christ came into the world so He knows how difficult it is to be yourself and make the choice to give consideration to what is right for you. The world pulled on Him to compromise Himself. Remember how Satan tempted Jesus to take a short cut when He was hungry and make bread out of stones? Then Satan tried to get Jesus to jump off of a very high place to prove that God would protect Him. When the first two didn't work Satan came back and offered Jesus the

[12] 1 Cor. 4:3–5

kingdoms of this world if He would bow down and worship him. See, Satan lies to you when you think the easiest way or the quickest way is the best for you. What the "World System" is saying to you is compromise yourself. This is how to destroy the material you have to be yourself and build your life.

Your temptations are very similar today because Satan is not very creative. He has always used the same tactics since he tempted Adam and Eve in the Garden of Eden. He uses your appetite for being in control and "in the know" to allure you away from letting God be your God. He also lies to you by telling you that you need the approval of others to say you are valuable. He wants you to think more about others opinion of you than what you know to be right for you. Satan goes for the basic human needs of love and acceptance to tempt you.

Notice that Jesus resisted the pull of the "World System" by coming back to God's Word. It is easy for you to test God and think you can do what you want and there will be no consequences. Jesus would not test God even though He knew He had all power. Jesus put worship and service together. He is saying that when you have a personal relationship with Christ you have a desire to walk the path that leads to abundant life.

You can be your own worst enemy. To prove that I want you to write down the ugly words or word you say to yourself daily. Do you ever call yourself stupid? This is a common practice and encouraged by the "World System." It is a lie you tell yourself and others reinforce by their behavior.

Your assignment is to make an acrostic on a separate sheet of paper and write down the negative word you say many times a day to yourself.

Example:
S _____
T _____
U _____
P _____
I _____
D _____

The next part of your assignment is to write a positive character trait by each one of the letters.

Example:
  Sincere
  Truthful
  Useful
  Patience
  Initiative
  Dedicated

When you call yourself stupid you do not have anything to work with that builds you up. When you look at your character traits you can build a healthy relationship. These characteristics are just beginning to develop in you so don't expect them to be 100%. You have a lifetime to grow them. It is the traits that you listed that will be used in the following chapters to help you put a contributing person into all of your relationships.

HEALTHY RELATING

Look at your character traits as a way to begin to discover what you have to offer to a relationship. Before you start a relationship it is good to look at what you want to bring to the association. Putting a character trait beside each letter of your ugly word you call yourself is a beginning. These character traits are things like honesty. It does not say you are one hundred per cent honest with everyone you meet. It does require however, you to have the desire to be an honest person and to be honest with yourself.

One of the problems encountered in trying to build a healthy relationship is taking responsibility FOR the whole relationship. You are only half of any relationship. You can only control your half of the relationship. Stop and recognize what you are responsible FOR. You and only You. You are responsible TO tell the other person the truth about who you are. You are not responsible for what they do with the information. **Do you want to take a heavy weight off of you when dealing with others? Only be responsible FOR yourself.**

You are totally responsible for yourself. You are the one you bring to the relationship. If you are happy, confident, and respectful of yourself, you have a better chance of success in relating to others. If you are down on yourself, always criticizing yourself, and comparing yourself with others you do not have much to give to a relationship.

When relating it is very important that you say who you are and what you have to give to the other person. This calls for defining the labels you wear. As you begin to define your labels such as; daughter, sister, or friend, you should know what you have to contribute to each one of these relationships. Looking back over the past pages you can clearly see how what is normal to you has been determined by what you have experienced in your life up to this point. If your "old normal" is what you want, that is fine. If you want to begin to establish your identity for yourself, then you must define for yourself the characteristics of the labels that you wear.

You usually start with the questions why am I here, what am I supposed to do or where do I fit in? These questions are out of order. The first discovery question is, **"How do I define the labels I wear with my characteristics?"** As a teen you more than likely have been labeled by others and not given respect

for what you think and who you are today. Now is the time
you to begin to change that and work from your perspective.

What are some of the greatest "labels" the world offers? You
can begin in Bible Times and think of King Solomon. He was
the richest and wisest man in the world. He had control of a
nation. He was the king. Yet all of his wealth and wisdom did
not fill the void in his life. Look at his writings in the book of
Ecclesiastes and seeing him saying, "All is vanity."

You might want to list people that are rich and famous
today. Is this the pattern for all of us? Is this the measure you
want to use to guide your life? If it is, you will remain puzzled
about your life because you are not that person nor do you have
the same resources they have to become who they are.

DEFINING IMPORTANT LABELS YOU WEAR

You wear many labels such as daughter, granddaughter,
sister, niece, girl friend, or student. The list can go on and on.

Who is responsible for defining the labels you wear? The
common answer to this is, "I am" but that is not what happens.
Usually the parents, grandparents, siblings, friends, pastors,
teachers, magazines, television, peers, movie stars and even
strangers tell you who you are supposed to be according to their
opinion on that day. All definitions need to be written by you.

DEFINITION OF DAUGHTER

**Your assignment is to look at who you are today as a
daughter.** A defining guideline is needed. It is time for you
to say who you are as the daughter of each of your parents.
You are the daughter and your character is what you have to
contribute to your mother and your father.

Everyone loses when labels go undefined by the person who
is wearing them. You are the daughter. It is necessary for you to
define what being a daughter is in relationship to your mother

or your father. Each relationship has a different definition.

You begin to define the daughter "label" by looking at who you are in relationship to one parent. It must be done individually because they are different people and you relate to them differently. If you treat them both the same it means you are not relating individually to them but you are performing to fit their combined standard.

Make a list of the labels you wear and as you read on. List the character traits and time you have to give to each relationship. You might want to list them in the order of importance to you.

Determine what you have to give to each relationship

    Time
    Energy
    Emotions
    Thought
    Presence

You were trained by many without realizing it. The way you talk, the way you greet people, the way you answer the phone, foods you like or dislike. The freedom to be yourself, I hope, but if not, you are where you can define the labels for yourself now. The following are a few examples for you to think about.

DEFINITION OF SISTER

As a sibling are you in competition with your sister or brother?

Are you measuring yourself by what they have accomplished or what they look like?

If they are older do you look up to them and learn from them?

If they are younger do you feel responsible for them?

How has this affected your relationship with each one of them?

DEFINITION OF CHRISTIAN OR DISCIPLE

Most people consider they are a Christian if they are born in the United States or have attended church. Some think it means to be a good person. Christians in New Testament times were called that to indicate they were followers of Jesus Christ. People were first called "Christians" in Antioch to indicate they were disciples of Christ. This name was given to those who followed Christ like the soldiers that served Caesar followed Caesar. It was a point of identity, or label, that others placed on them because of their loyalty to Christ.

In today's world the name Christian has a watered down meaning. To be a disciple means you are a learner and a follower of Jesus Christ. The message Jesus gave His disciples before His resurrection was—

Go therefore and make disciples of all the nations, baptizing them in the name of the Father and the Son and the Holy Spirit, teaching them to observe all that I commanded you; and lo, I am with you always, even to the end of the age. [13]

Notice that Jesus said make disciples (followers) not make Christians. They were told to be responsible FOR giving the message Jesus had given them. The Good News. They were also instructed to teach and to train them when they had accepted Jesus.

DEFINITION OF FRIEND

It is dangerous to let others tell you who you are supposed to be as a friend. What they have said to you affected your early opinion of who you are. Now is the time for you to decide what you have to give to each friendship. You are responsible FOR you and only you. **Do you mean I am not responsible for**

---

[13] Matt. 28:19–20 The Message

anyone else but me? Yes. You cannot control another person. You only have control of yourself. You have responsibility TO others. What that means is that you give what you have to them in the area that you are trying to build with them. In God's Word we are told to love one another. That means that I need to be patient with the other person and kind to them. That is something I can give TO them. It is not something I can make them give to me. God only holds you accountable for your own life. He is very interested in you sharing your life with others in a healthy connection that builds both of you up and encourages you.

Here is a diagram that will help if you are a visual learner.

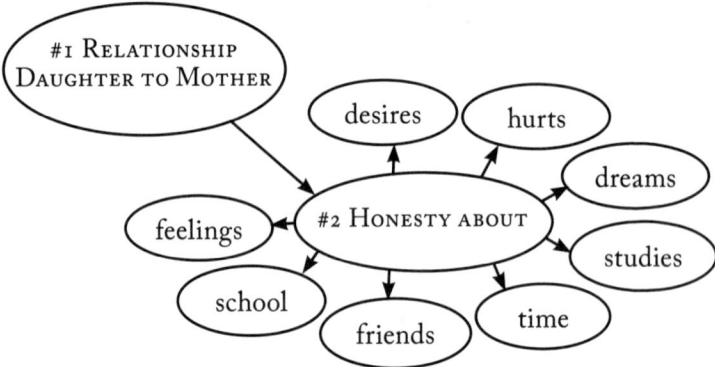

The first circle tells you which relationship you are working on.

The second level is a characteristic you want to put into the relationship.

Some characteristics you might want to consider are:
   Trustworthy
   Responsible
   Respectful
   Fair
   Caring

The third level is what you need to be honest about.

Do you see how this says who you are and what you are giving to the relationship?

HOW TO DECIDE WHICH WAY IS RIGHT FOR ME

No one ever told me how to decide which way is right for me. **Do you feel you are caught between two opinions or two life styles?** I know you are being pulled in two directions. That is the feeling of everyone who is trying to learn who she is. It seems we have a standard that most people accept and we will call that the "World System." The "World System" teaches you how to please everyone around you but it does not help you to learn who you really are. It makes you one of a group without the ability to express your uniqueness.

Then there is the invitation God has offered you to be able to have eternal life and abundant life here and now. Jesus' invitation is *I am the way, and the truth, and the life; no one comes to the Father, but through Me.*[14] This invitation is to know who God is and to know who you are and how valuable you are to Him as an individual. This becomes the foundation on which you can build your identity securely.

Accepting the invitation to be rightly related to God is a choice that you make. It is an individual choice, not a group choice. Everyone makes the choice to believe God is telling the truth or that He is lying. To make the choice not to believe Him means eternal separation from God. Jesus says,

> *"Enter by the narrow gate; for the gate is wide, and the way is broad that leads to destruction, and many are those who enter by it. For the gate is small, and the way is narrow that leads to life, and few are those who find it."*[15]

Look at the two roads of choice. It helps to have the two roads in front of you when you make the choice. If your choice

---
14 *John 14:6 NASU*
15 *Matt. 7:13–14 NASU*

is to go through the Narrow Gate that leads to Eternal Life it will show in your actions. The big questions is, **Do you want Eternity with God or do you want the instant gratification that comes from approval from the crowd on the Broad Way and separation from God eternally?**

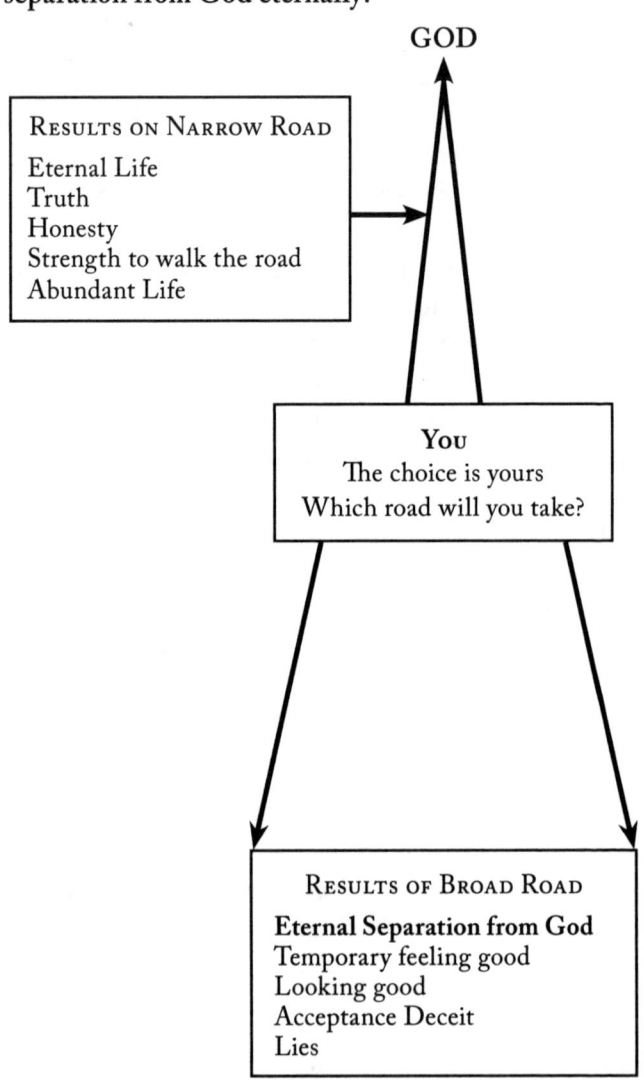

Since Christ died for all people and all are invited to come to Him, it is unfortunate that only a few accept the invitation. If you are going to follow Christ you can count on being in the minority. You can also count on being fulfilled and happy with your life. He does not promise that everything will work out smoothly for you but He does promise to walk with you, never leave you, and give you the strength to follow. The Apostle Paul put it this way.

> *I know how to get along with humble means, and I also know how to live in prosperity; in any and every circumstance I have learned the secret of being filled and going hungry, both of having abundance and suffering need. I can do all things through Him who strengthens me.* [16]

Since you live in this world it is very difficult to see the advantages of such a long view as eternal life. Eternal life is a hard concept because we cannot grasp something being endless. You can go for the material life because that means you can have all of the good things of life now. It sounds like instant gratification doesn't it? The pull on you is to seek the plentiful life by the "World System." Since the majority of the people in our world are not interested in what God says about making life rich and meaningful it is very important that you know as much as you can about who God is and who you are.

Before you can look at how to walk the narrow path that leads to life and resist the pull of the "World System" that leads to destruction you need to discover who you are today with an inside view. The things you say "Yes" and "No" to at this time of your life can affect the rest of your life. I hope you are beginning to get a picture of how important you are to God and how much you really matter to Him.

In order to have a better understanding of eternity let's

---

[16] *Phil. 4:12–13 NASU*

begin before the beginning. You have a choice to make a new belief system that is all yours. You have looked at how your belief system has been formed up to this point in your life. Now let's take a new look at who God is and get acquainted with Him. Jesus Christ said He came to explain God to us. (John 1:8) I want you to take special note of what God is offering you to work with in your life and how much value He has placed on you.

God speaks in His word and says He wants a personal relationship with you above all else. *He chose us in Christ before the foundation of the world...*[17] It is an awesome thought that God, Christ and the Holy Spirit made a plan of redemption for us before the world was created! He wanted a relationship with you so He made it possible. It is His desire to relate to you on a personal basis. Since He is God and He knows everything from the beginning to the end He cared enough to plan for you. He wanted to relate to you one on one in a personal way. His PLAN for you is that you accept His invitation to build a personal relationship with Him that will last throughout eternity.

What do you mean when you say a person is a believer in Jesus Christ?

> It means to believe God is who He says He is and has done what He says He has done for you.
>
> It means to believe what He says in the Bible enough to trust Him with your eternal life and learn to walk with Him as an expression of love for Him.

When you accept Him personally you are given eternal life right then. You are an eternal being right now. You have Eternal life without end with the Holy Spirit as your guide. He has your best interest in mind.

Has it occurred to you that the plan of redemption for your salvation was planned before the earth was ever created? Since

---

17 *Eph. 1:4 NASU*

God wanted to be able to relate to you personally He planned how the relationship would work. He knew what was going to happen in the Garden of Eden with Adam and Eve. It was no surprise to Him. He gave them choice. **Have you ever thought how important choice is?** Without choice it would be impossible to have a personal relationship. We would be robots.

He knew how much He cared for them even though they made the mistake of choosing to try to be equal with Him. He made mankind with the power to choose even when the choice may be to go against Him. How precious it is to God when you choose to relate to Him with your own free will. He invites each one to come to Him.

God does not automatically control you. He is not in the automaton business. Part of the benefit of being made in the image of God is that we have the power to make choices. This is a gift from God. With choice comes responsibility. You cannot blame others for the choices you make. Adam tried to blame God and Eve for his mistake. Eve blamed the serpent. God made each one of them responsible FOR their own decision.

God gave Adam and Eve the gift of choice. They could eat of all of the trees in the garden but one. Eve was tempted by Satan when he promised she could know good and evil. Up until then she had only known that which was good. See how she was trapped by seeking instant gratification? The tree was good for food, it was delightful to look at and she desired it because she was promised it would make her wise. She lost her innocence and learned quickly what rejecting God meant. Now she was ashamed and hid thinking covering herself with leaves would hide what she had done. **Do you suppose they thought they could keep this a secret from God?**

It was God who sought Adam and Eve after they disobeyed. It was not Adam and Eve who tried to find God. Now they had become afraid of God. They hid from God because fear had entered their lives.

God is the one who provided clothing for them because they were ashamed when they recognized they were naked. God is the one who offered them a renewed relationship with Him by seeking them. He also protected them from living eternally in separation from Him when He moved them out of the garden away from the Tree of Life.

You may be saying, "Yeah, I know the story. **What does that have to do with me?**

Adam and Eve are only a part of the story. God chose a people who were later called Israel to represent Him and we see their history in the Old Testament. The Israelites were chosen by God to reveal to the world what a relationship with God looks like. He provided for His people and moved them out of 400 years of slavery in Egypt into the Promised Land. As long as they chose Him as their God they were blessed and provided for. He always warned them where the dangers were and told them how to travel with Him. When they chose their own way they suffered the consequences. When they followed Him they had a protective covering.

Throughout the Old Testament we have the history of how God walked with a few of His people. It was never the masses that followed God. Yet God had a plan of deliverance that He carried out in His faithful followers. He has always given people a choice to let Him be their God or choose their own way (idols). The majority chose idols instead of a relationship with God even though it meant their destruction.

The story becomes even more personal when you see God's revelation of Himself in Christ. From majesty to manger the journey was to reveal who He is and how He desires to relate to each one. Can you imagine what it must have been like for Jesus to come out of heaven into this dirty world? Jesus did this to let you know how important you are to Him. He wants you to understand who God is and the price He was willing to pay to reach you. There is no price tag you could ever put on what it cost Christ to make it possible for you to come to God through His sacrifice for you.

5

WHAT DOES GOD WANT FROM ME?

WHAT GOD WANTS FROM ME

It helps to look back through history and see how God has been misrepresented. In much of the church's history there has always been what were called "false teachers."

> *My dear friends, don't believe everything you hear. Carefully weigh and examine what people tell you. Not everyone who talks about God comes from God. There are a lot of lying preachers loose in the world.*
>
> *Here's how you test for the genuine Spirit of God. Everyone who confesses openly his faith in Jesus Christ—the Son of God, who came as an actual flesh and blood person—comes from God and belongs to God. And everyone who refuses to confess faith in Jesus has nothing in common with God. This is the spirit of antichrist that you heard was coming. Well, here it is, sooner than we thought!* [18]

False teachers were defined as people who were trying to undermine the Good News of the gospel by adding to it. They wanted to make it something that you do instead of a personal relationship with Him. People who deny the Good News are all around you. In order to understand how to relate to God it is necessary to get acquainted with God from what He says about Himself and not what others think about Him. Even though the world does not listen to you about God because of their unbelief you have overcome the world's message because of your trust in Christ.

What does relating to God mean? Let's try to define the word relating from God's perspective and then maybe we can better understand how it works. God wants only the very best for you. Look at what it means to relate to God. To relate means: association—friendship—connection—involvement. He calls you a friend and wants to be involved with you as a trustworthy FRIEND. In the New Testament, Jesus and His disciples illustrate the growth of friendship from that of teacher and disciple, lord and servant, to that of friend and friend.

> *I've loved you the way my Father has loved me. Make yourselves at home in my love. If you keep my commands, you'll remain intimately at home in my love. That's what I've done—keep my Father's commands and made myself at home in his love.*
>
> *I've told you these things for a purpose that my joy might be your joy, and your joy wholly mature. This is my command. Love one another the way I loved you. This is the very best way to love. Put your life on the line for your friends. You are my friends when you do the things I command you. I'm no longer calling you servants because the servants don't' understand what their master is thinking and planning. No, I've named you friends because I've let you in on everything I've heard from the Father.* [19]

To relate means: connection—unite—join—attach—belong. Look at how much He talks about unity and being one with Him.

---

[19] John 15:13–17 NASU

The Spirit himself testifies with our spirit that we are God's children. Now if we are children, then we are heirs-heirs of God and co-heirs with Christ, if indeed we share in his sufferings in order that we may also share in his glory. [20]

To relate means: rapport—understanding—empathy—link—bring together—tie—bond. Joint heir with Him. Thomas said to Him,

"Lord, we do not know where You are going, how do we know the way? Jesus said to him, I am the way, and the truth, and the life; no one comes to the Father but through Me. [21]

Looking at all of these scriptures gives more information to help answer the question, "How does the relationship with God work?" He says over and over in His word that what He wants is a personal relationship with you. Your part of connecting with Him is accepting Him for who He is and believing He did what He said He did just for you. He died for you. He made it possible for you to get acquainted with Him by His personal word, the Bible, and His Holy Spirit, who is your teacher and helper to support you here and now. He values you more than you will ever be able to understand.

To build a healthy association you have to get acquainted with the person you are trying to relate to. Think of someone you have a good relationship with.

What qualities make that connection strong?
To relate means you have a sense of belonging, a feeling of being accepted by the other person. Now it would be a good time to decide what you really know about who God is from His Word. The Apostle Paul tells a secret that has been hidden

[20] *Romans 8:16–17 NASU*
[21] *John 14: 5–6 NASU*

> from the beginning of time. He introduces us
> to God in Christ. The Apostle John had already
> quoted Jesus as saying that He is the only way to
> God when He said, *"I am the way, the truth, and
> the life and no person comes to God except by Me."* [22]

Trust is very important in building a relationship. To trust God you must know Him.

In the book of First John we find how important it is to know His word, but it is not enough to just know His Word. Satan knows the Word of God but He does not accept it. You believe that God is one. *You do well; the demons also believe, and shudder.* [23]

Have you taken a personal look at what Christ did for you on the cross?

> *So we have stopped evaluating others by what the world thinks about them. Once I mistakenly thought of Christ that way, as though he were merely a human being. How differently I think about him now! What is means is that those who become Christians become new persons. They are not the same anymore, for the old life is gone. A new life has begun!*
>
> *All this newness of life is from God, who brought us back to himself through what Christ did. And God has given us the task of reconciling people to him. For God was in Christ, reconciling the world to himself, no longer counting people's sins against them. This is the wonderful message he has given us to tell others. We are Christ's ambassadors, and God is using us to speak to you. We urge you, as though Christ himself were here pleading with you. "Be reconciled to God!" For God made Christ, who never sinned, to be the offering for our sin, so that we could be made right with God through Christ.* [24]

---

22 John 14:6 NASU   24 2 Cor. 5:16–21 NLT
23 James 2:19 NASU

You have a new beginning in Christ. All of your past is where it belongs, in the past. He not only gave you a new life but He will not hold you accountable for your prior rejection of Him now that you have chosen Him. He has given you Eternal Life. He took care of sin in your life. He added something else; new life. He then invites you as His daughter to be His representative to the world. He chooses to speak through each person as they choose Him.

> *Therefore, we are ambassadors for Christ, as though God were entreating through us; we beg you on behalf of Christ be reconciled to God.*
>
> *He sees you as righteous because of your decision to choose Him.*
>
> *He made Him who knew no sin to be sin on our behalf; that we might become the righteousness of God in Him.*[25]

It is important that you see that Christ provided righteousness for you, not perfection. The world tells you because you are not perfect you cannot relate to God. That is a lie. It is because you could not be perfect that Christ died for you and He provides your righteousness.

When you believe God, He goes a step further and gives you the privilege of being His representative on behalf of Christ to those around you. He lets you carry this special message of Good News and He is the one that does the convicting of sin. All He asks of you is that you walk with Him and represent Him by letting others know what His invitation is to them.

Remember what is yours when you walked through the Narrow Gate to Eternal Life. This passage should give you a security that makes a very safe place for you with God. When you accept Jesus Christ as your Savior you become

---

[25] *2 Cor. 5:17–21 ASV*

a new person to Him. The rebellion against God as God is gone and He made you a new person belonging to Him. **Do you understand that He is not holding you responsible for your sin of rejecting Him? Does that sound too good to be true?** It is awesome and true. Only God loves with that kind of love. It is called grace. He paid the price for everyone's sins for all time. The unfortunate thing is that many people do not believe Him enough to trust Him with their Eternal Life. The choices in life are: believe God is who He says He is and did what He said He did to make a personal relationship with you for your benefit OR work your own life out by the "World System" which is controlled by the one who is called a liar, deceitful, evil, and only wants to steal from you, destroy you and eventually kill you. When you look at it that way it looks like an easy choice.

What are some of the lies the "World System" tells you?

> Is it that possessions are very valuable to happiness or that fun and pleasures are very necessary to your happiness? If it feels good now it must be right. Money equals value. This is what the "World System" tells you.

Jesus said,

"I am the door; if anyone enters through Me, he shall be saved, and shall go in and out, and find pasture. The thief comes only to steal, and kill, and destroy; I came that they might have life, and might have it abundantly." [26]

You may be saying, "Yeah, **where is my abundant life?**" It will take time for you to see the comparison between your life before Christ and now because the "World's System" has such a strong hold on you. Since you were born into a world of instant gratification it is a big change to follow what Christ says and

---

26 *John 10:9–10 NASU*

let Him direct your path. I want you to remember that there are only a few who find the path to Eternal Life because the glitter of the world is so appealing. I recently heard of a young man who after drinking alcohol for a number of years decided it was not the life for him any longer. He went into rehab and with the help of many people walked a straight path for two years. One day he ran into difficulty and instead of turning to God returned to alcohol. It killed him quickly. This is a picture of how Satan is in the business of stealing, destroying and killing. It is easy to have a picture of Satan as a little red devil who is just mischievous instead of who scripture says he is.

> *Keep a cool head. Stay alert. The Devil is poised to pounce, and would like nothing better than to catch you napping. Keep your guard up. You're not the only ones plunged into these hard times. It's the same with Christians all over the world. So keep a firm grip on the faith.* [27]

Because Jesus lived in this world, He understands where we live and what it is like to live in the world. Temptation comes when you waiver between what God says in His Word, which is best for you and what you think or what others think is best for you. This is every Christian's battle. **Will you follow what He says or will you do what you want to at the time?** Notice that when you are tempted He has provided a way out so you are not overcome.

> *No test or temptation that comes your way is beyond the course of what others have had to face. All you need to remember is that God will never let you down; he'll never let you be pushed past your limit; he'll always be there to help you come through it. So, my dear friends, when you see people reducing God to something they can use or control, get out of their company as fast as you can.* [28]

---

27 1 Peter 5:8-9 The Message
28 1 Cor. 10:13 Message

It is a choice to trust that Christ wants the best for you. Do you think that you know what is best for you? Because God values you so much when temptations come to you He provides a way for you to get through it and come out victorious. Some of those choices come when you are tempted to say something mean instead of an encouraging word. It could be when you are displeased and you are tempted to attack the other person's character instead of speaking up for yourself. The "World System" says lie and cheat to get what you want. Jesus says to tell the truth and to not cheat to get what you want.

6

LET GOD SPEAK FOR HIMSELF

WHAT MAKES A SECURE IDENTITY?

Security is a major priority in the world today. Whether it is personal, national or global everyone is concerned. It is very important to have accurate information about those people around you. To survive the pressures of your world it is a must to have accurate information about who God is. You cannot rely on hear-say from testimonies, books, DVD's, opinions or Sunday school stories. It is so easy to operate on assumed information or what you have heard from others. Do not believe something to be true about someone else unless it comes from the person. Everyone screens or adds to information they are given by others. It is their opinion and not necessarily the truth.

You must have the truth about God from God's word. He is TRUTH. *I am the way, <u>the truth</u> and the life and no person comes to God but by me."* [29] When you believe what God says about loving you and wanting the best for you it clears up the distortion of what you have believed about Him and yourself. It is unfortunate the number of people who see God as trying to take something from them instead of trying to give them encouragement and help.

Before you look at how you can know that God wants the best for you, it is important to learn how the information fits you. Understanding is a process. When you understand one

---

[29] *John 14:6 NASU*

area there is still more to learn. Understanding a truth moves you to a more personal depth in your link with God.

Here are some questions to ask yourself when you are reading God's word.
- **What does this passage say about God?**
- **How personal am I willing to let Him be to me?**
- **Am I willing to trust Him enough to receive His acceptance of me?**
- **What is my part?**
- **Do I believe God is telling the truth?**
- **Can I do anything to help my understanding?**
- **Do I believe that God allows time for me to understand and practice what I learn?**

Putting what you have learned into practice makes the information yours to use.

Will you give yourself time to establish your own convictions? Convictions are different than knowledge. Having a conviction means you have confidence, certainty, assurance, sincerity about your belief. When you are persuaded by His Word it is becoming your belief or conviction. This brings about your maturing into a young adult who truly believes what God says.

In order to establish your own belief system we will study the first chapter of the book of Ephesians. It is something you can live by your entire life. As you understand it you will have a guideline to follow. I studied this passage several years ago for six weeks with a young person. We have discussed it often in these past years. Last week I received a call and he said, "I can't believe all of the new things I am discovering as I reread this scripture. It is like a diamond mine that you can continue to explore and find even more treasures."

The Apostle Paul was writing to the Ephesian Christians as a church to make known the mystery of God's will to them.

He probably wrote from Rome during his imprisonment about 25 years after Jesus was crucified. He had established the church in Ephesus on his second missionary journey and spent three years with them. He was in contact with them two other times. His journeys are recorded in Acts 19.

As we make this journey together, my desire is that you will learn to listen to what is being said as a personal word to you.

What is your perception of the will of God?

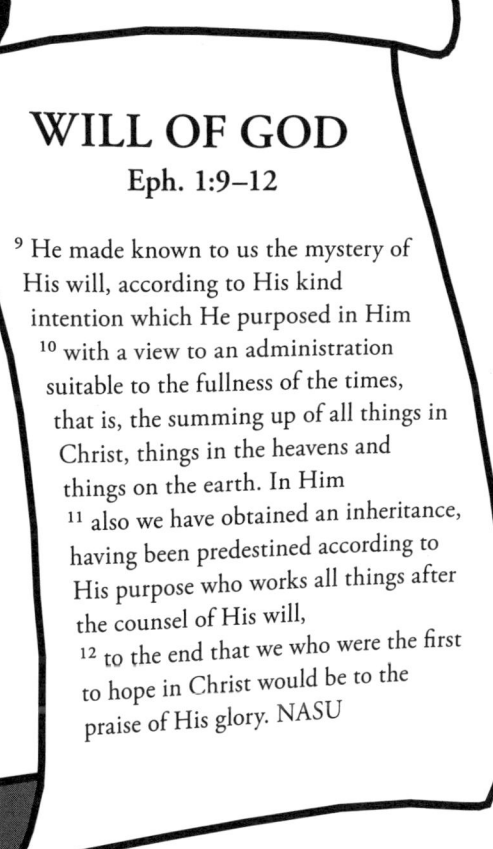

WILL OF GOD
Eph. 1:9–12

⁹ He made known to us the mystery of His will, according to His kind intention which He purposed in Him ¹⁰ with a view to an administration suitable to the fullness of the times, that is, the summing up of all things in Christ, things in the heavens and things on the earth. In Him ¹¹ also we have obtained an inheritance, having been predestined according to His purpose who works all things after the counsel of His will, ¹² to the end that we who were the first to hope in Christ would be to the praise of His glory. NASU

A description of a will is a document that is drawn up by a person who has something they want to give to another when they die. It is often referred to as a "last will and testament." God's will is spelled out throughout the Bible. We are going to concentrate on what God says He is providing in the death of Jesus Christ. God's will is that each person come to Him IN Christ.

> *Now when someone dies and leaves a will, no one gets anything until it is proved that the person who wrote the will is dead. The will goes into effect only after the death of the person who wrote it. While the person is still alive no one can use the will to get any of the things promised to them.* [30]

The standard treatment of the will of God for life in the eyes of many believers goes something like this. It is so trivial as thinking God makes special parking spots available for you when you want. Or it may be to have the traffic light change to green before you get there so you will not have to stop. Sometimes it is who you are to date, what dress you are to wear to the prom, where you are to go to school, or not letting it rain on your picnic. This thinking makes God driving every car, flying every plane, in charge of every gun and causing everything that happens. There is a big difference in God knowing everything and God doing everything. Is God interested in all of these things? He is if you are. However, He is not moving everything around to make your life easy or without decisions you are to make. He is not controlling the universe so you can have sunshine today. Everyone has choice. Choice is a God given gift.

Repentance is involved in coming to God. It is turning from you directing your life to letting Him be your God. God directs your life through His word and His Spirit. It is your choice to follow. Remember a relationship has two parts

---

[30] Heb. 9:16–17 NLT

because there are two people involved. God has done His part and He invites you to come to Him trusting Him to adopt you into His Kingdom. He trusts you to choose to walk with Him.

Some of the things God is in control of.
- The plan of salvation before the foundation of the world
- His creation
- Holding on to your salvation
- Your protection from evil overcoming you
- When the end of time will be
- You may want to add to this list as you begin to get better acquainted with God.

Your security comes from knowing God and what He has provided for you. God made possible our relationships to Him described in Hebrews. In Ephesians His desire (will) is for us to accept His gift to us and relate to Him.

WHAT GOD'S WILL IS FOR ME

A will describes what God has spelled out as your inheritance when you choose to let Him be your God. It is an act or process of volition, specifically, a wish, desire; longing; inclination; disposition; pleasure. It is something wished by a person, especially by one with power or authority to carry it out. The Apostle Paul reminds the Church at Ephesus that God's will was laid out before the foundation of the world to be IN Christ.

In Ephesians 1:9 it means "the gracious design" rather than "the determined resolve." What a difference! The design says that what you are made for is to relate to Him. His will is not a command to you but what He wants for you to receive from Him. He wants to give you Eternal Life and then help you find Abundant Life here and now.

A *will* becomes active at the death of the person who makes it. Since Christ is a part of the making of the will, His death

...e your inheritance available to you here and now. The ...ostle Paul lists some of what is included in the inheritance. The final part of your inheritance will only become available when you see Jesus in heaven.

If His *will* were a 'determined resolve' it would mean that there is a mystery out there that you must solve and you had better get it right before you can receive it. **Why would God try to trick you? Why would He try to teach you a hidden lesson when you find it difficult to listen to the plain and simple direction in His word?** He makes it plain that His *will* is in your accepting Christ as your way to God.

There is a big difference in working to try to make something happen and expressing gratitude for what you understand you have been given. Trying to make something happen makes it all your responsibility. Expressing gratitude for what you have received involves a giver (Christ) and a receiver (you).

WHAT MY INHERITANCE IS

The way to answer the question of your inheritance is to study Ephesians to see how valuable you are to God.

Ephesians 1*

1 Paul, an apostle of Christ Jesus by the will of God, to the saints who are at Ephesus, and who are faithful in Christ Jesus:

This tells you who wrote the book (Paul) and to whom it was written (the believers in Ephesus).

2 Grace to you and peace from God our Father and the Lord Jesus Christ.

Grace and peace are gifts from God and Christ. Look at the

---

* Ephesians passage is from the NASB usless otherwise stated.

meaning of these two words.

GRACE is God giving you something that you need but cannot earn, deserve, or provide for yourself.

PEACE. Jesus said He is your Peace or that you have peace with God through Him. This peace means to be bound together with Christ in an indissovable living union because of the price He paid for your sin. Peace comes from God our Father and the Lord Jesus Christ through the Holy Spirit. It is an inside job. It does not mean all is going well in your world. It comes when you trust Him that what He wants is to help you find abundant life right where you are. Do not think of peace in the world because peace happens in each individual's life as Christ is believed. **Does this seem impossible from where you are today?**

*3 Blessed be the God and Father of our Lord Jesus Christ, who has blessed us with **every spiritual blessing** in the heavenly places **IN Christ**,*

What does a spiritual blessing look like to you?

You do not have to wait for every spiritual blessing. He says He HAS (past tense) blessed you with every spiritual blessing IN Christ. All of your blessings are coming to you in your relationship to Christ. These come to you as you begin to listen, believe, and trust Him. Paul makes a list of some of your inheritance. **In the following verse list the blessing from Him to you.**

*4 just as **He chose us IN Him** before the foundation of the world, that we should be **holy and blameless** before Him. In love.*

This plan was made before the world was formed. God's plan was to make a way for you to relate to Him. That plan would include the way He chooses to look at you. He sees you as HOLY, set apart, and BLAMELESS in His eyes. You probably do not have anyone in your life that looks at you as blameless because you are not perfect. **Do you see that God is not asking for perfection but that you understand how much He loves you and wants you to receive His love without conditions?** We have a tendency to think of blessings as the times when everything is going well for us or something is happening that is good for us.

5 He predestined us to adoption as sons through Jesus Christ to Himself, according to the kind intention of His will,

Here it is again, His kind intention toward you. His *will*. It is preplanned by God Himself. When someone tells you that God is causing harm or hardship to you to teach you a lesson you should look carefully at this verse. He made the plan to adopt you as a daughter of His through Christ and that was according to the kind intention of His *will*. His *will* is a total concern on your behalf. He is for you not against you. He only wants the best for you. **Do your believe this for yourself?** His plan is to lead you into abundant life. He wants you to enjoy the relationship with Him and not be afraid.

6 to the praise of the glory of His grace, which He freely bestowed on us IN the Beloved.

Your adoption as a daughter indicates how He is reaching out to you. His grace is offered to you through Christ. This gift was at great cost to Him but freely given to you. His love for you is expressed IN Christ. His love is His love not something you earn. It becomes active in your life when you receive it. **Are you one of many people that cannot accept this gift because you think that if you are freed from guilt you would perform poorly?** That is not true. The more you accept what Christ has done for you the more you want to walk with Him.

7 IN Him we have redemption through His blood, the forgiveness of our trespasses, according to the riches of His grace,

IN Christ you have had your sins paid for in full. If you saw the movie, The Passion of Christ, or have studied the crucifixion you have a little better picture of what it cost Christ to pay for your sin. He paid it all. There is no installment plan. There is no more payment to be made. In this transaction there is freedom to relate to God and your errors are covered by the richness of His grace. No one likes to be around someone who requires them to qualify by their standard before they accept them. Christ is not. **Have you accepted what He has done for you? Are you aware of the freedom He is trying to give you?**

8 which He lavished upon us.

He has furnished this forgiveness to you in excess knowing full well that you would need it as you moved through your life. Keep in mind it is not perfection God is seeking but He loves you so much He wants to be with you and help you through a world that is totally against Him and you.

In all wisdom and insight

9 He made known to us the mystery of His will, according to His kind intention which He purposed IN Him

Almost everyone likes a mystery to be revealed. Sometimes you are tempted to turn to the end of the book to see how it ends. God is gracious. He declared the secret of His *will* IN Christ to the church at Ephesus and you are included because of His kind intentions toward all who come to Him. You must remember that the Christians at Ephesus were Gentiles not

Jews. The Jews saw them as heathens and felt they could have no part with God. IN Christ all of this changed because the invitation was opened to the whole world. God wanted everyone included. Remember we studied the scripture that says,

> *All this newness of life is from God, who brought us back to himself through what Christ did. And God has given us the task of reconciling people to him. For God was in Christ, reconciling the world to himself, no longer counting people's sins against them. This is the wonderful message he has given us to tell others. We are Christ's ambassadors, and God is using us to speak to you. We urge you, as though Christ himself were pleading with you. Be reconciled to God! For God made Christ, who never sinned, to be the offering for our sin, so that we could be made right with God through Christ.* [31]

Do you see why God says you are righteous IN Him?

> *10 with a view to an administration suitable to the fullness of the times, that is, the summing up of all things IN Christ, things in the heavens and things upon the earth.*

Christ has come and provided salvation for you. Hear the good news. He came at just the right time and He will come again at just the right time. In His coming to die for you there is an inheritance that is yours now. Remember this was all pre-planned by God before the world was created. It is in believing what He is saying to you that helps you experience abundant life.

IN Him

11 also we have obtained an inheritance, having been predestined according to His purpose who works all

---

[31] *2 Cor. 5:18–21 NLT*

things after the counsel of His will,

Verse 11 lets you know that God has a purpose and *will* for you. Because He has it laid out IN Christ this is not something that you have to continually be searching for. Your efforts need to be placed on accepting what is said to you personally and living as an adopted daughter of the King. When you understand this there will be a desire to follow His word as an expression of your love and appreciation for who He is to you.

12 to the end that we who were the first to hope IN Christ should be to the praise of His glory.

Nothing glorifies or praises Christ more than you believing what He says about how much He loves you and what He has provided for you in His dying for you. This calls for an expression to Him of what this means to you. That expression is made by the way you live your life following His Word.

7

GUARENTEED SECURITY

WHERE DOES SECURITY COME FROM?

Security is the big word today. Everywhere we go there is someone checking something to make us safe. There are security checks at stores to be sure there is no stealing. There are luggage checks in airports to protect from terrorists. Packaging for products is everywhere for protection from tampering. We live in a world where more and more people are living by their own code of conduct which gives them permission to do as they please. This is in a different form today than when the Apostle Paul wrote to the Ephesians of the first century but the hearts of people have not changed. When every person feels free to write their own guidelines apart from God's Word, evil will be the mode of the day.

Paul addresses where real security comes from and what it looks like to the believer.

> *13 IN Him, you also, after listening to the message of truth, the gospel of your salvation—having also believed, you were sealed IN Him with the Holy Spirit of promise,*
>
> *14 who is given as a pledge of our inheritance, with a view to the redemption of God's own possession, to the praise of His glory.* [32]

This is the way it reads in the New Living Translation

13 And now you also have heard the truth, the Good News that God saves you. And when you believed in Christ, he identified you as his own by giving you the Holy Spirit, whom he promised long ago.

14 The Spirit is God's guarantee that he will give us everything he promised and that he has purchased us to be his own people. This is just one more reason for us to praise our glorious God. *

You cannot even begin to know all that is yours in Christ's inheritance but let's at least look at what we can understand to this point. There are two requirements: (1) you must listen to the Good News and (2) you must believe what He says is true for you. When you have believed, absolutely nothing can take you out of God's hands. His promise has a guarantee. He holds on to you. It is not your performance or good works that keep you secure in Him. It is His doing. He is the provider of Eternal Life. This is not something you can make happen. God has provided your redemption. He offers it to everyone, and it is yours to accept or reject. When you have accepted His provision for you He is the only one who can secure it for you. He keeps it in a safe place IN Christ.

I want you to notice how many times Paul refers to our inheritance being IN Christ for each believer. Remember that a believer is one who trusts Christ enough to let Him say what He has provided and accepts it enough to let Him be the guide for her life. A guide is one who assists a person in traveling through or trying to reach a destination in an unfamiliar area. Isn't it wonderful to have this offer of help? **Are you beginning to get the picture as it applies to you?**

Add to the list of the references to IN Christ.

v 2   from Christ

---

* *Eph. 1:13–14 NLT*

v 3 has blessed us with every spiritual blessing
v 5 made a plan of adoption through Jesus Christ
v 6 to the praise of the glory of His grace, which He freely bestowed on us IN the Beloved.
v 7 IN Him we have redemption, forgiveness, according to the riches of His grace
v 8 lavished upon us
v 9 made known the mystery of His will, according to His kind intention which He purposed IN Him
v 10 Summing up all things IN Christ, things in the heavens and things upon the earth,
v 11 IN Him we obtained an inheritance, purpose and counsel
v 12 we who were the first to hope IN Christ should be to the praise of His glory
v 13 IN Him heard the message of truth—sealed IN Him with the Holy Spirit of promise
v 15 I have heard of the faith IN the Lord Jesus which exists among you, and your love for all the saints
v 19–20 in accordance with the working of <u>the strength of His might</u> the <u>surpassing greatness of His power toward you</u> which He brought about IN Christ.

HOW TO CONNECT WITH GOD

Everyone needs to learn how to pray. Even Jesus' disciples asked Him to teach them how to pray like John had taught his disciples. It is good to study the prayers in scripture to learn how to pray. If you are not careful you will pray like those around you pray instead of studying how prayer is used in the Bible. God wants a personal relationship with you. **To be personal means you must talk to God about you.** It is you that He wants to guide. He has not made the whole world your assignment. He works with you where you are. He asks that you be his disciple or learner and His ambassador where you are. **Try praying for yourself.** It may be more difficult than you think.

Look at how personal He wants to be with you. Learn from Jesus as He prays.

Then Jesus prayed this prayer:

> *"O Father, Lord of heaven and earth, thank you for hiding the truth from those how think themselves so wise and clever, and for revealing it to the childlike. Yes, Father, it pleased you to do it this way!* [33]

Then He begins to talk with those around Him. This is His part of the relationship.

> *My Father has given me authority over everything. No one really knows the Son except the Father, and no one really knows the Father except the Son and those to whom the Son chooses to reveal him.* [34]

His invitation to you is the way He reveals himself to you.

> *Come to Me, all who are weary and heavy-laden, and I will give you rest.*

Your part.

> *Take My yoke upon you and learn of Me,*

He tells you who He is, what He will do and the results.

> *for I am gentle and humble in heart, and YOU WILL FIND REST FOR YOUR SOULS. For My yoke is easy and My burden is light.* [35]

You have had the opportunity to know who Jesus is and what He has done for you. He invites you to learn and understand who He is from Him not from someone else. His

[33] Matt. 11:25-26 NLT
[34] Matt. 11:27 NAS
[35] Matt. 11:28-30 NAS

teaching is gentle not harsh. He has come from the majesty and glory of heaven to explain to you who God is. He offers you balance when He tells you to take up the yoke. The yoke was used to connect two oxen together so they might pull a loaded cart or plow a field. For the yoke to work the two had to pull together. One could not go ahead of the other without injuring both animals by rubbing their hide until it was raw and neither could work. When the two pulled together the cart or burden is easy to bear. I saw this demonstrated when I was on a mission in Peru. Jesus is offering to walk at your pace while you are learning from Him.

Back to Ephesians 1. The Apostle prays for the believers in Ephesus.

15 For this reason I too, having heard of the faith IN the Lord Jesus which exists among you, and your love for all the saints (believers),

16 do not cease giving thanks for you, while making mention of you in my prayers;

Paul saw the evidence of the Ephesians faith in the way they expressed their belief in Christ by love for other believers. He was very thankful for the way the believers lived out what they said they believed. The way you express your belief in what Christ has said is shown in the relationships you build with other believers. You are taught in the following verses how to pray for yourself and others. See how prayer is mainly about you and God.

17 that the God of our Lord Jesus Christ, the Father of glory, may give to you a spirit of wisdom and of revelation in the knowledge of Him.

He prays for the spirit of wisdom and of revelation in

the knowledge of God. **What does this mean now? Does wisdom come with the asking or do you need to be involved?** Wisdom is having a deep perception or discernment and sound judgment based on the Word of God.

> *"And in religion the "wise man" is he who gives to the things of God the same acuteness that other men give to worldly affairs."* [36]

Revelation means information that is newly disclosed, especially surprising or valuable. The revelation is letting them become fully acquainted with what was theirs in Christ. His desire was that their knowledge or full discernment be acknowledged in their lives.

He saw the evidence of the Ephesian's faith and understanding in the way they expressed their belief in Christ by love for other believers. The more personal the relationship with Christ, the more genuine your expression is to others. **How have you seen this demonstrated?**

> *18 I pray that the eyes of your heart may be enlightened, so that you will know what is the hope of His calling, what are the riches of the glory of His inheritance in the saints,*

An enlightened heart is one that sees clearly what is being said to her. The more understanding you have of the message of your inheritance, the more you are free to express who you are in Christ. He wants you to be aware of the hope His invitation has for you. He wants you to consider how all of this works out in your day to day life. The hope also includes a confidence in all of your future. Christ often emphasized His return to call His followers to Himself.

There is an abundance of dignity and honor in being an heir of the King. Look at the privilege that belongs to you.

---

[36] Luke 16:8 (from *International Standard Bible Encyclopedia*)

When you receive it for yourself you can willingly give to others. How about that? The inheritance that is IN Christ is distributed to the world in the believers who accept it from Him. We get to give the message of all of His wealth to those around us. **Are you aware that all of the spiritual blessings mentioned are to be delivered by the "saints" (you and me)?** In the New Testament "saint" refers to a follower of Christ. God allows us to do His work here and now.

> *19 and what is the surpassing greatness of His power toward us who believe. These are in accordance with the working of the strength of His might*

I do not think your mind can comprehend what kind of power is there for you when you believe God is who He says He is. It is God who provides all of this for you it is not something you make up for yourself. The scripture says,

> *Abide in Me, and I in you. As the branch cannot bear fruit of itself, unless it abides in the vine, so neither can you, unless you abide in Me. I am the vine, you are the branches, he who abides in Me, and I in him, he bears much fruit, for apart from Me you can do nothing.* [37]

What is it that we can do nothing about? Is everything left up to God? No, you are involved. There is nothing you can do to be right with God other than to abide in Him. To abide means that you know what His word says. You accept what He says about what He has done for you. He gives you the strength to carry on in a "World System" that is opposed to you and what you believe.

> *20 which He brought about IN Christ, when He raised Him from the dead, and seated Him at His right hand in the heavenly places,*

---

[37] *John 15:4–5 NAS*

21 far above all rule and authority and power and dominion, and every name that is named, not only in this age, but also in the one to come.

If you want to know the cost of all of the power He has spent on you just look at what Christ paid for you to be able to have a relationship with God. The one crucified now sits in the heavenly places. He is there for you.

He is the victor. He has overcome the evil one. *Be of sober spirit, be on the alert. Your adversary, the devil, prowls around like a roaring lion, seeking someone to devour.* (1 Peter 5:8 NASU) You are safe because the payment for your rejection of God has been paid. You have accepted Christ as your way to God. His warning is for you to be alert and knowledgeable about what is going on around you that is trying to rob you of your abundant life.

22 And He put all things in subjection under His feet, and gave Him as head over all things to the church,

23 which is His body, the fullness of Him who fills all in all.

These words of the Apostle Paul tell us how powerful Christ is and that He is relating personally to the believers, the church, where He has chosen to operate in this world. The church is the body of believers who choose to come together and remember what Christ has done for them. They also gather to encourage and care for one another. Do not judge the church by the person who professes with their mouth and does not live their life following Christ. Christ is our Savior, example and strength. Find those people who have a personal relationship with Christ that shows as your right example of what the church is. Be a person who makes Christ believable because of the way you follow Him.

WHAT MY RELATIONSHIP TO CHRIST PROVIDES FOR ME

We have studied the abundance of what we have available to work with in relationship to Christ and there is even more. But before we look at more, the Apostle Paul reminds us of where a person stands without Christ.

Ephesians 2

> *1 And you were dead in your trespasses and sins,*

Without Christ's intervention for you there is no hope for eternal life with Him.

> *2 in which you formerly walked according to the course of this world, according to the prince of the power of the air, of the spirit that is now working in the sons of disobedience.*

One of the most common questions is, **"Why does God let Satan be the prince of the power of the air in this world?"** Look at how Satan works. He is working in the sons of disobedience. Satan can do nothing to the believer because you are sealed IN Christ. All Satan can do is lie, deceive, steal, destroy and kill eternally a soul that is not protected IN Christ. **Think of ways Satan has lied to you. Has he tried to convince you that you are not "good enough" for Christ to love you? Has he tried to deceive you by tempting you to compare yourself with others? Is he destroying your value by self criticism?**

Each person chooses whom they believe. You either believe Christ or you do not believe Him. If you choose not to believe you are being deceived by Satan that there are no consequences for your decision.

Do you realize how much God wants to relate to you? He provided redemption for you before He created the world.

What does that say to you about His desire to relate to you? Look at one of the scriptures that you have already learned.

> *For God so loved the world that He gave His only Son, so that everyone who believes in Him will not perish but have eternal life. God did not send the Son into the world to condemn it, but to save it. There is not judgment awaiting those who trust him. But those who do not trust Him have already been judged for not believing in the only Son of God. Their judgment is based on this fact. The light from heaven came into the world, but they loved the darkness more than the light, for their actions were evil. They hate the light because they want to sin in the darkness.* [38]

Notice that God is not there to judge you but to provide salvation for you. Do not run away from Him.

The next question is, **"Why doesn't Jesus just come and end all of this now if He is the victor?"**

> *The Lord isn't really being slow about His promise to return, as some people think. No, he is being patient for your sake. He does not want anyone to perish, so He is giving more time for everyone to repent.* [39]

Do these scriptures help you to answer the question? The opposite of good is evil. The opposite of light is darkness. The opposite of obedience is disobedience. It is either serve Christ or serve the devil who operates the "World System." It is either follow truth or follow lies. Here choice is again to be exercised.

> *3 Among them we too all formerly lived in the lusts of our flesh, indulging the desires of the flesh and of the mind, and were by nature children of wrath, even as the rest.*

---

38 *John 3:16–20 NLT*
39 *2 Peter 3:9 NLT*

9 not as a result of works, that no one should boast.

If grace could be earned, a comparison with others would happen. We would always be trying to excel more than others. **If grace was a result of works could you see the competition with others happening?**

10 For we are His workmanship, created IN Christ Jesus for good works, which God prepared beforehand, that we should walk in them.

We have the privilege of doing God's work because of our relationship to Him. He wants the very best for you and always has. Remember back in the first chapter of Ephesians He said all of His Spiritual Blessing are in the Saints; you and me. You are in partnership with Him as a believer.

8

HOW THIS WORKS FOR ME

WHAT BEING IN CONTROL MEANS

Who is in control anyway? You may answer, "I have no idea." Let's look at how control works. What are you in control of? You probably would say, "Very little." It seems that parents are in control at home, teachers are in control at school or that others in your daily life seem to call the shots.

Parents have a God given assignment to instruct you, love you, and teach you but you are in charge of what you do with the information. Teachers give you assignments but you are in charge of whether you learn or not. Your peers may ask you to do something but it is up to you to decide what is best for you.

As a Christian you may not want to take responsibility and simply say, "God is in control." You will hear this statement often in the Christian world. Is it just an easy answer to keep you from studying and really knowing God for yourself? Look back at what He says His *will* is for you. He has only "kind intentions" toward you so He would not do anything to hurt you. When you take a wrong path the only way to learn from it is to turn to God's Word and let Him direct you toward abundant life. Consequences may be there but He restores your confidence and helps you move on.

God has the power to do whatever He wishes. Since this is true it would be a good study to just look at the things

God chooses to use His power to control.

Just think of the power it takes to keep the earth, moon, stars, and sun in place.

He keeps each believer secure in Him.

He is doing His part in relating to you.

He is always available to you.

He dwells in each believer.

He provides light for your path.

He picks you up and dusts you off when you stumble.

Continue thinking about what He does with His power.

Begin your list of things God says He does.

If He controlled you there would be no place for you to decide about the relationship. When you look at what He says, God invites you to believe in Him, trust Him and follow a path that leads to abundant life. It is yours to choose what you will do. God does not decide that for you. He invites you to be in relationship with Him but it is yours to make your mind up about what you want to do and how connected you want to be to Him. He does not use circumstances to force you into following Him. Look around you at all of the bad circumstances and look at the people who choose to blame God and become bitter instead of asking God how to get through this period in their life.

Take a look at King David and how he made a choice to look at the beautiful woman, Bathsheba bathing, and then sending for her to come to him in his palace. He had intercourse with her and she became pregnant. In order to try to cover up his sin he sent to the battlefield for Uriah, her husband, hoping he would come home to her and think the child was his. Uriah came, at the King's commander, but would not go home because his troops were still fighting. He returned to battle without sleeping with his wife, Bathsheba.

David ordered his general, Joab, to put Uriah on the front

line of battle and not protect him so he would be killed. He was trying to cover his sin. After Bathsheba's time of mourning was over David sent for her to become his wife.

Nathan, the prophet, came to David and told him a story about a rich man who had many lambs taking the only lamb of a poor man and killing it for a feast for his guests. After King David heard the story he was ready to have the rich man killed for what he had done.

Nathan then said to David, *"You are the man!"* Then Nathan proceeds to tell David what will happen to him and his household. Then David said to Nathan, *"I have sinned against the Lord."* And Nathan said to David, *"The Lord also has taken away your sin; you shall not die. However, because by this deed you have given occasion to the enemies of the Lord to blaspheme, the child also that is born to you shall surely die."* You can read this complete story in 2 Samuel 11–12 (NAS).

The picture of how God relates to us is very plain when you look at King David. When confronted by the prophet, who was a spokesman for God, David repented. He realized he had done all of this in front of God and against God. His repentance brought forgiveness to David.

BUT he suffered the consequences of his actions. Nathan told David that because of his sin he had given occasion to the enemies of the Lord to blaspheme. The children of Israel were to give a picture of who God is to the rest of the world. David's sin gave the enemies of the Lord reason to disbelieve God. David's household was in a state of confusion for the remainder of his life.

Do you see how important it is that you do your part? God is there for you when you are ready to relate to Him on His terms. There is room for choice. Please don't confuse God knowing all things with God causing all things. He knew what David had done but He did not cause David to sin.

HOW DOES THIS BEGIN TO WORK FOR ME?

Putting others in control of your life says you do not want to accept the responsibility for your decisions. To begin the work means you must take responsibility FOR yourself. You choose. It is a day by day adventure you are on and you get to choose your path. But what does the scripture mean when it says *"he will direct my path?"* [40] This Psalm helps you to understand that *His word is a lamp to your feet and a light for your path.* He makes the path well marked by His Word. It is your choice to do the walking according to His direction in His word. If you decide to take side trips off of the lighted path don't blame God. You decided.

You are a unique individual. This is not a group decision. You are whole in Christ so it is unnecessary for you to seek from others what seems right for you. If the God of this universe trusts you enough to let you make choices for yourself that is impressive. **Why don't you take Him up on His offer?**

The answer comes back, "But you don't know me." **Did God invite you to come to Him when you got your life all worked out and everything was perfect?** NO. The scripture teaches that the only way to come to God is by believing He is who He says He is and He did what He said He did for you. **Does being blameless and holy before God seem like an impossible dream?** Yes, but it is who He is. He means what He says. He wants you to understand He truly is God come down to die for you. He has made it possible for you to be right with Him. This is something you cannot do for yourself. Remember it is a gift.

I often talk with people who believe that God is who He says He is but cannot believe that He includes them in the invitation to come to Him just as they are. **How can this be true when He says so much about personally relating to you?** God accepting you as you are is very difficult to understand because you do not see it very often in your family, circle of

---

40 *Psalm 119:105 NAS*

acquaintances and friends. Everyone from parents to strangers expect you to be who they think you should be.

Can you think of someone who tries to get you to be someone they want you to be? When you fail to measure up to their expectations then they often leave you out or take something you care about away from you. Because this is their pattern it is easy for you to place this measure on God when you try to relate to Him. **Do you think of Him always correcting or punishing you for being who you are?** It is very difficult to think of Him as caring for you just like you are but He says He does.

Are you drawn to a person who tries to make you over to be what they want you to be? It usually causes you to withdraw from them completely because you feel like a failure. Many times Christ is described as a person who is dissatisfied with you the way you are. If you often hear how you are to make yourself like Him or you need to strive to please Him so He will be happy with you and it causes discouragement. I read the invitation to "Come to Him and relate to Him." He is not asking for behavior modification but for a relationship. He wants you to get to know Him for who He is and to relate to Him as you are today. It is not a relationship about who you will become but based on who you are today. He is not concerned about tomorrow but today. God works in your today not tomorrow or yesterday.

> *But seek first His kingdom and His righteousness; and all these things shall be added to you. Therefore do not be anxious for tomorrow; for tomorrow will care for itself. Each day has enough trouble of its own.* [41]

What does it mean to stay in today? You are throwing today away if you try to work in yesterday and correct things there. It may be necessary for you to review your past to heal

---

41 *Matt. 6:32-33 NASU*

injuries that occurred there. This is true if they are hindering your today. It is also needless to try to work in tomorrow because it is not here yet. He asks you to work in your today.

It is very easy to look around and think everyone else is having an easier time trying to relate to God than you do. Remember to relate to someone means to belong to each other with a feeling of acceptance. God says He accepts you just as you are today. Do you accept Him for who He says He is today or are you still trying to figure out what you are supposed to be doing? Doing all of the right things does not necessarily make a relationship. Sometimes we substitute church attendance, Bible study, and other church activities instead of looking in His Word in order to get acquainted with Him. These could be "check marks" to say you are a "good Christian." Knowing Him is much more than that.

The stumbling block is that accepting yourself as you are today sounds arrogant. Many times we are misinformed by well meaning people when they quote the scripture that *you are not to think of yourself more highly than you ought.*[42] This is talking about being puffed up and comparing yourself with others and thinking you are better than they are. The Apostle Paul asks that you have sound judgment and really look at who God is and how much He desires a relationship with you instead of thinking of yourself as having arrived.

Before the instruction is given not to overrate yourself the Apostle Paul invites you to make a present of yourself to God. Give Him the gift of relating to Him in a personal way. He says this is an act of worship or another way of saying this is the way you express yourself that you truly believe He loves you as He says He does. This transformation begins in your mind. It concerns your belief system. Instead of what you were told throughout your life by others how about working off of God's information. Their opinion is only their opinion not the

---

[42] *Romans 12:3 NAS*

truth about you.

God's message is true and it is,

> *So here's what I want you to do, God helping you. Take your everyday life—your sleeping, eating, going-to-work, and walking-around life—and place it before God as an offering. Embracing what God does for you is the best thing you can do for Him. Don't become so well-adjusted to your culture that you fit into it without even thinking. Instead, fix your attention on God. You'll be changed from the inside out. Readily recognize what he wants from you, and quickly respond to it. Unlike the culture around you, always dragging you down to its level of immaturity, God brings the best out of you, develops well-formed maturity in you.* [43]

These verses let you know what God is to you. He invites you and desires you to look at the mercy which is His kindness and *good will* toward you with a desire to relieve you from worrying about the right performance. He invites you to bring yourself to Him as a vital alive present to Him. You are holy in His sight because you have accepted what He said about who He is to you. This is the primary way that we worship Him—being present in the relationship to Him.

He also lets you know where you can get tripped up by fashioning yourself according to the "World's System." Instead, He says the way to be successful is to change your mind by examining the truth about what you believe about you and God. The more you understand that His *will* is His desire or pleasure for a personal relationship with you the more you can relate to Him personally. His gift of Himself to you is perfect. He offers Himself completely to you. Your gift to Him is accepting Him as He says He is and being honest and real with Him.

---

[43] *Romans 12:1–2 The Message*

HOW TO MAKE WHAT GOD SAYS WORK

Have you been through a time in your life when what you understood about God did not work for you? I have. I prayed for health, no pain, healing, and life for my late husband yet he was in unbearable pain and he died. **Where was God? Does He just sit there and do nothing? Why is He so silent when I am in such pain?**

Part of growth is to question God because of all that is happening to you. If you do not have any questions you are not trying to understand God in a personal way. God loves for you to seek answers by questioning His word and studying it for yourself to make it personal.

When the question haunts you, **"If God loves me so much why has my life been so miserable?" Why hasn't He stopped all of the bad? Where do you turn?** The only way to answer these questions is to see what God has to say to you about what He is interested in most. He does not promise to be a pain reliever. The healing that He does is inside out if you will listen to what He is providing for you minute by minute.

When all of this does not seem to be working for you my question is, **"Are you measuring from the "World System?"** Here is a check list to help you to begin to understand how the "World System" measures.

Is "People pleasing" your goal?
> Who do you try to please most?
> Is satisfying people the answer?
> Do they like you more?
> Do they accept you and build you up?
> How long will they be happy with you?
> What is in it for you when you "people please?" Are you being real when you are people pleasing or are you a pretender?

Think about these questions because it is impossible to

please someone all of the time. They change wha[t]
from you at any given time. "People pleasing" is co[mpromising to]
this world pattern. It is denying who you are and h[oping the]
other person will like you as a pretender.

If your goal is to please others more than to be the real person you are you are compromising.

The following are compromising trends.

Comparing yourself with others in:

        Appearance   Popularity
        Weight   Material things
        Height   Physical pleasures
        Clothes   Esteem
        Complexion   Power
        Grades

What do you see as your greatest struggle in this list?

Let's look at what comparison causes…

Be real. Movie stars' photographs are digitally enhanced and altered to create a digital fantasy version of them. Comparison with them puts you in an unfair place. Are they real? Look at their lives. Do you want the emptiness that calls for alcohol, drugs and multiple relationships that end in divorce or death? Look at the whole picture.

Test yourself

- Are you allowing others to control you? How? This takes the form of giving in to what others think when that is not what you believe. It can be going along with things you know are wrong in order to be accepted. When you compromise what you really believe does it make you happy?

- When you let others control you are you letting them be god to you? By that I mean does doing what they say carry more weight with you than what God says?

All of the above are efforts to get your needs met to feel secure, accepted and loved. They only work for a short time if at all. Compromising your belief system only makes you feel guilty and unloved.

What does scripture say our greatest needs are?

They must be to be secure, accepted and loved because the scripture is full of assurances that God has provided just that for you. This can happen in today's world but it involves your relationship being personal with God. **Does everything have to be visible to you for it to be real?** If it does then you cannot use your cell phone because you cannot see all that is going on as you talk with a friend.

Check your beliefs about God.

What does God do and what is your responsibility in relationship to Him?

Some other scriptures you can explore to know God better.

We have all heard someone say God does not give you more than you can handle. Look at what scripture says.

> *If you think you are standing strong, be careful, for you, too, may fall into the same sin. But remember that the temptations that come into your life are no different from what others experience. And God is faithful. He will keep the temptation from becoming so strong that you can't stand up against it. When you are tempted, he will show you a way out so that you will not give in to it.* [44]

- God is not the tempter
- Temptations are lies to deceive you. It is what the world does to try to get you on the broad path to destruction.
- The deception is in the idea that everyone is doing it.
- The thought that it is just impossible in today's world to relate to God. I can't be perfect so why try?
    I can't have fun without going along.

[44] 1 Cor. 10:12–13 NLT

I will be left out.
What will it hurt just once?
- Since Christ dwells in you by His Holy Spirit you can make it through the temptation without yielding to it. God will tell you the truth if you will listen.
- God will always show you a way out so you can stand strong.

Is any of this easy? No, it requires a strong belief system in the fact that God means what He says and He is really there for you offering to help you.

Most of the time God is thought of as the one who is there to provide whatever you ask for. The ask, seek, knock in Luke is used to imply God is supposed to act because that is what you want.

So I say to you, ask, and it will be given to you; seek, and you will find; knock, and it will be opened to you. For everyone who asks, receives; and he who seeks, finds; and to him who knocks, it will be opened. And so I tell you, keep on asking, and you will be given what you ask for. Keep on looking and you will find. Keep on knocking, and the door will be opened. For everyone who asks, receives. Everyone who seeks, finds. And the door is opened to everyone who knocks. [45]

It is important to read his illustration that follows in order to understand what he is talking about. He uses the example of parents giving to children.

You fathers—if your children ask for a fish, do you give them a snake instead? Or if they ask for an egg, do you give them a scorpion? Of course not!

The understanding of the text comes in the next verse.

---

[45] Luke 11:9–10 NLT

> *If you sinful people know how to give good gifts to your children, how much more will your heavenly Father give the Holy Spirit to those who ask him.* [46]

He is teaching us to desire the relationship with Him above all. Ask for it. Seek it. Knock on doors until you find out more who He says He is.

It would be good to study the entire chapter of Luke 11 so you can understand what is being said. It is easy to start with the idea that if you ask and keep asking, seek and keep seeking and knock and keep knocking God is obligated to do what you want. Sometimes it gets as ridiculous as asking God to keep it from raining on your parade.

Another big question is, **why does God takes someone in death when they are so young?** God does not "take" a person. He receives them when they no longer have a body that will support them.

The answer depends on who you want to listen to.

> *So Jesus said to them again, "Truly, truly, I say to you, I am the door of the sheep. All who came before Me are thieves and robbers, but the sheep did not hear them. I am the door; if anyone enters through Me, he will be saved, and will go in and out and find pasture. The thief comes only to steal and kill and destroy; I came that they may have life, and have it abundantly. I am the good shepherd; the good shepherd lays down His life for the sheep.* [47]

Satan is the thief and in charge of this "World System" through people who serve him. Satan's desire it to steal from you your full life in Christ. He is there to kill you with all of the things that God is warning you against. His whole objective is to destroy you. All of the things that kill people

---

46 Luke 11:11–13 NLT
47 John 10:7–10 NASU

are done by people who decide they know more than God knows. Death came into the world in the Garden of Eden because of sin.

> *Therefore, just as through one man sin entered into the world, and death through sin, and so death spread to all men, because all sinned.* [48]

Sin is rebellion toward accepting God for who He says He is and rejecting what He has done to relate to you. Satan, the thief, destroyer, and killer does not want you to believe what God says to you. **Do you trust a liar? Do you trust your belongings to a thief?**

God, on the other hand is there to provide Eternal Life and to fulfill your desire for a full and meaningful life. He can be trusted because He keeps His word. If you feel He does not I would challenge you to study it and be sure who is right.

The next thought is, "But God is all powerful and He could stop the disease, accident, or whatever if He wanted to." **That is true but is that what He promises to use His power for?** He is interested in your relationship to Him. He is providing your eternal destiny as well as trying to direct you to a meaningful life here and now. The Apostle Paul helps to clarify why death comes.

> *For we know that when this earthly tent we live in is taken down—when we die and leave these bodies—we will have a home in heaven, an eternal body made for us by God himself and not by human hands. We grow weary in our present bodies, and we long for the day when we will put on our heavenly bodies like new clothing. For we will not be spirits without bodies, but we will put on new heavenly bodies. Our dying bodies make us groan and sigh, but it's not that we want to die and have no*

---

[48] Romans 5:12 NASU

bodies at all. We want to slip into our new bodies so that these dying bodies will be swallowed up by everlasting life. God himself has prepared us for this, and as a guarantee he has given us his Holy Spirit. [49]

When your body (tent) can no longer support you in this world God has provided a heavenly body for you. This is part of the security that God provides for you. You are an eternal person. God cares for you.

When you accept what Christ has done for you personally you become "light and salt" to your world around you. It is light that dispels darkness. Darkness cannot put the light out because the light overcomes it. It makes an interesting study to look at the number of times light is mentioned in the New Testament. Walking in the light keeps you from stumbling.

You have the Holy Spirit to teach you the truth about God. He is not in you to torment and convict you but to encourage you.

But now I am going away to the one who sent me, and none of you has asked me where I am going. Instead, you are very sad. But it is actually best for you that I go away, because if I don't the Counselor (Encourager) won't come. If I do go away, he will come because I will send him to you. And when he comes, he will convince the world of its sin, and of God's righteousness, and of the coming judgment. The world's sin is unbelief in me. Righteousness is available because I go to the Father, and you will see me no more. Judgment will come because the prince of this world has already been judged.

Oh, there is so much more I want to tell you, but you can't bear it now. When the Spirit of truth comes, he will guide you into all truth. He will not be presenting his own ideas; he will be telling you what he has heard. He will tell you about the future. He will bring me glory by

---

49 *2 Cor. 5:1–5 NLT*

revealing to you whatever he receives from me. All that the Father has is mine; this is what I mean when I say that the Spirit will reveal to you whatever he receives from me. [50]

This passage lets you know how interested Christ is in you. He wants you to know the truth so you can be guided in your life and have understanding about life. The Holy Spirit is also there to be your Helper.

The Apostle John says,

I write this, dear children, to guide you out of sin. But if anyone does sin, we have a Priest-Friend in the presence of the Father: Jesus Christ, righteous Jesus. When he served as a sacrifice for our sins, he solved the sin problem for good—not only ours, but the whole world's. [51]

The Spirit is there to encourage you and remind you what Christ has already done for you and how He continues to be there to guide you by His word.

In my opinion one of the most irresponsible statements a Christian can make is, "Well, just accept your loss because God is in control."

WHAT CONTROL LOOKS LIKE IN SCRIPTURE

The word "control" is not a positive word in the Bible. It is a common thought that is heard often that God is in control of almost anything that a Christian talks about. It is one thing to say that God is Supreme and another to say He is in control.

Jesus said, I will not speak with you much longer, for the prince of this world is coming. He has no hold on me, but the world must learn that I love the Father and that I do exactly what my Father has commanded me. [52]

---

50 *John 16:5–15 NLT*
51 *1 John 2:1–2 The Message*
52 *John 14:30–31 NIV*

Jesus also makes a statement, *Judgment will come because the prince of this world has already been judged.* [53]

In other New Testament passages the word archon, "a potentate," "a person in authority," "a magistrate," occurs. In most of these instances the term "prince" refers to the devil.

SOVEREIGNTY OF GOD is a theological term which refers to the unlimited power of God, who has sovereign control over the affairs of nature and history. A better word is Lord God. The Bible declares that God is working out His sovereign plan of redemption for the world and that the conclusion is certain. [54]

It is important to see how God made the plan for redemption before the foundation of the world and He will do what He said He would do to save you and keep you.

The word "control" in the New Testament has a prefix. It is self-control. It is a positive thought when it is self-control because that means you are following the direction of Christ in your life. The purpose is to relate to you where you are as you are. He wants to help you though His word and His Spirit.

> *But the fruit of the Spirit is love, joy, peace, patience, kindness, goodness, faithfulness, gentleness and self-control. Against such things there is no law. Those who belong to Christ Jesus have crucified the sinful nature with its passions and desires. Since we live by the Spirit, let us keep in step with the Spirit.*
>
> *Let us not become conceited, provoking and envying each other.* [55]

GOD LETS YOU CHOOSE

He lets you choose to accept Him or reject Him.
He lets you choose what you want to do with your life.
He lets you choose to walk with Him or not walk with Him.
He lets you choose to love others as He loves you or miss

---

53 *John 16:11 NLT*
55 *Gal. 5:22–26 NIV*
54 *From Nelson's Illustrated Bible Dictionary, Copyright © 1986, Thomas Nelson Publishers*

the abundance of life.

He gives you resources. His Holy Spirit, His Word, other believers, He doesn't leave you alone.

WHAT REALLY COUNTS IN LIFE TO YOU?

What does the pursuit of Abundant Life look like to you?

The rich and plentiful blessings of God are accessed by connection, involvement, listening, being heard, affirmation, and trust. All of these attributes build you up and help you live your life in a more meaningful way.

9

REINFORCING MY VALUE

HOW TO REINFORCE THE VALUE GOD PLACES ON ME

Look at what you have to work with
You: Imperfect material, but blameless in God's eyes
Parents
Siblings and friends
Talents
Skills
Learning ability
School and teachers
Church
Friends
A God who loves you just the way you are.
What are you saying, "Yes" to in your decision making? The "Yes" things are laid out in scripture that help you in all of your choices. Say, "Yes" to what God says. Here is one example.

> *It was He who gave some to be apostles, some to be prophets, some to be evangelists, and some to be pastors and teachers, to prepare God's people for works of service, so that the body of Christ may be built up until we all reach unity in the faith and in the knowledge of the Son of God and become mature, attaining to the*

> *whole measure of the fullness of Christ. Then we will no longer be infants, tossed back and forth by the waves, and blown here and there by every wind of teaching and by the cunning and craftiness of men in their deceitful scheming. Instead, speaking the truth in love, we will in all things grow up into him who is the Head, that is, Christ. From him the whole body, joined and held together by every supporting ligament, grows and builds itself up in love, as each part does its work.* [56]

Say "Yes" to things that build you and others up not things that tear down. Be interested in unity by believing what God has said is true. This requires knowing His Word. As you practice working with the positive truth you will grow up to a healthy individual.

Knowing God's word keeps you from being pushed around here and there by other's opinions. It helps you to recognize manipulation and deceit when you see it.

It helps you speak truth, be genuine and real.

It helps you be a healthy part of the family and the church. Here is an example of what you need to say, "No" to.

> *So I tell you this, and insist on it in the Lord, that you must no longer live as the Gentiles do in the futility [immorality] of their thinking. They are darkened in their understanding and separated from the life of God because of the ignorance that is in them [no knowledge of who God is] due to the hardening of their hearts. [stupidity, callousness] Having lost all sensitivity, [feeling] they have given themselves over to sensuality [filthy living] so as to indulge in every kind of impurity, with a continual lust for more. [practicing evil to get better at it]*

---

56 *Eph. 4:11–14 NASU*

Put on the New Self.

> *You, however, did not come to know Christ that way. Surely you heard of him and were taught in him in accordance with the truth that is in Jesus. You were taught, with regard to your former way of life, to put off your old self, [pattern of living] which is being corrupted by its deceitful desires; to be made new in the attitude of your minds; and to put on the new self, created to be like God in true righteousness and holiness.* [57]

The way to put on the new self is to change your thinking from following after the "World System that is around you. The new thinking is that you are created in righteousness and holiness of the truth. Learn to believe all of this about yourself.

It is very easy to confuse righteousness with perfection. So much of what God has for you is missed if you think being perfect is the goal. The righteousness does not come from your doing everything right it comes as a gift from God when He takes away your sin. He replaced your sin with His righteousness when you accepted Christ as your way to God. God looks at you as righteous and holy. These are two conditions that can only be provided by God. He offers them to everyone but it only benefits those who take Him seriously and believe what He says enough to trust Him to walk with Him.

What you need to be saying "Yes" to. The way you put on the new self.

No lies—only truth.

Be angry—tell the truth in love when displeased.

Don't sin by holding on to your anger—stuffing it or denying you are displeased.

Accept responsibility for what you are experiencing. Your feelings of anger are coming off of your belief system about what you are supposed to be in control of.

---

[57] *Eph. 4:17–24 NAS*

No stealing—the mode of the day in Bible times was take what you want just like it is today in the 'World System" without Christ as your guide.

Work so you have something to give to those in need—share out of what you have not necessarily what others want.

The importance of self-control.

Self-control is the way you are able to say "Yes" and "No" at the correct times. Self-control is a fruit of the Holy Spirit.

> *But the fruit of the Spirit is love, joy, peace, patience, kindness, goodness, faithfulness, gentleness, self-control; against such things there is no law. Now those who belong to Christ Jesus have crucified the flesh with its passions and desires. If we live by the Spirit, let us also walk by the Spirit. Let us not become boastful, challenging one another, envying one another.* [58]

Look at what is working inside of you. As you continue to walk with Christ as your guide the Holy Spirit is developing:
- love that comes from God
- joy which is a cheerfulness, calmness and gladness
- peace in the form of quietness and confidence in Him
- patience which is fortitude and long suffering
- kindness which is exhibited in gentleness, usefulness, and moral excellence
- goodness which is a virtue and tenderness
- faithfulness is truth itself
- assurance is authenticity
- gentleness practices meekness and humility
- reliance on Christ for salvation
- self-control or temperance

All of the qualities of the fruit of the spirit are not things that you must perform but are character traits that are being developed in your life as you continue to build

---

58 *Gal. 5:22–26 NASU*

your relationship with Christ. Often the phrase is used that someone wants Christ to make them to be like Him. I see this as your assignment and it is carried out as you look to what Christ has said in His word as your guide for living.

The desire to do evil is gone because you are no longer enemies of Christ. The focus of your life is in the opposite direction of evil. This does not mean that you are perfect and that you do everything right. What it does mean is that you do not practice habitually going against what God's word says.

The Apostle James gives one of the ways you can exhibit self-control.

> *For we all stumble in many ways. If anyone does not stumble in what he says, he is a perfect man (mature person), able to bridle the whole body as well. Now if we put the bits into the horses' mouths so that they will obey us, we direct their entire body as well. Look at the ships also, though they are so great and are driven by strong winds, are still directed by a very small rudder wherever the inclination of the pilot desires. So also the tongue is a small part of the body, and yet it boasts of great things. See how great a forest is set aflame by such a small fire! And the tongue a fire, the very world of iniquity; the tongue is set among our members as that which defiles the entire body, and sets on fire the course of our life, and is set on fire by hell.* [59]

The illustration of a horse and ship being controlled by something small make a strong point. What you say is important. The tongue is a small part of the body but can be deadly in the form of exaggeration or gossip. Gossip is a destroyer of you and others. Watch your mouth. Control what you say. Tell the truth. Only talk about yourself and what you have experienced. No adding to what is true. Let others tell

---

[59] *James 3:2–6 NASU*

what they want about who they are. That is not your job.

Sometimes it seems there are too many rules to remember on top of daily living. I think that is the reason Jesus simplified it by getting to the main point when He answered the Pharisees and Sadducees testing Him about the greatest commandment. He said,

> *To love the Lord your God with your heart, and with all your soul, and with all your mind. This is the great and foremost commandment. The second is like it, You shall love your neighbor as yourself. On these two commandments depend the whole Law and the Prophets.*[60]

What does this mean to love God with your whole person?

How does this work? **Ask yourself how you express your love to your family and friends?** When you love someone it is important to consider what they say and express yourself to them honestly. **Do you hear what God says to you in His word? Is it important enough to you for you to respond to Him?**

What does a healthy relationship with God look like?

There is an axiom that goes around in the Christian community that says the way to relate to God is Jesus, Others, and You which spells JOY. Look at the scripture again.

It says:
- We are to love God with our whole being.
- We are to love others as we love ourselves

Diagramed it would look like this;

JESUS ⟶ OTHERS ⟵ YOU

This would mean that others are between me and God.

60 Matt. 22: 37–40 NASU

Wrong! **Is this where we get the idea that we are answerable to others instead of listening to who God says we are?**

It says: Love God with my whole being. As I receive His love for me I can love others.

JESUS ⟷ YOU ⟷ OTHERS

It is confusing to have voices coming from every side telling you what you need to be doing and how perfect you need to be. A picture is needed that will help you decide how to achieve what you want to put into the relationship. You also need to think about what you want to get out of it. **What are the guidelines?**

It is important to realize that Christ has provided the strength for you to do whatever is necessary in relating to Him. *"I can do all things through Him who strengthens me."* [61]

Here He is giving to you again. **Who does the work and who gives the strength?** Almost everyone wants Christ to do the work and they will give the strength. It is the reverse. He gives the strength but you do the work. You talk simply with Him about you and how you can be victorious with His strength.

Conversations you can have with Him:
- What you need to do in a particular situation
  (Remember you do the deciding on the basis of what you know about what He has already said to you in His Word.)
- Listening to what He says is best for you.
 (This says whether you really believe He is for you.)
- What I can do to build the relationship from my side
- Understanding what you bring to the relationship.
- How much time you want to put into the relationship.

God's desire is shown in giving you the opportunity to relate to Him. He is reaching out to you. His invitation is for you to come to Him.

---

[61] Phil. 4:13 NAS

It is importance to know yourself and value yourself before you can build relationships. No one wants to take a person they do not like into a relationship. It is necessary for each person to learn to value herself as God values her.

How much does it take for Christ to convince you that He values you just the way you are?
- More creation?
- Dying again on the Cross?
- Sending miracles every day?
- Answering your every request with a "Yes"?

We must look like the child who sits under the Christmas tree with a hundred gifts, crying for more, when she has not opened the first one. God loves you. Probably one of the first songs you learned as a child was *Jesus Loves Me* but for some reason His love is not accepted. You will only be able to relate to God as much as you believe what He says to you. He loves you.

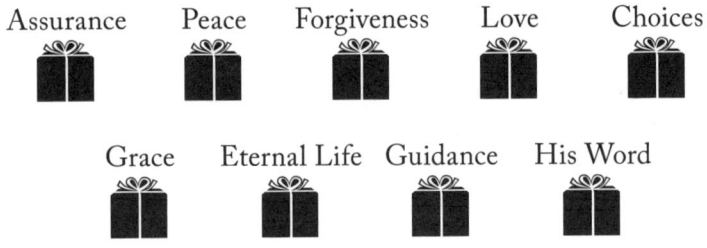

Do you believe God needs to do more to prove Himself?

10

COMMUNICATING ME

HOW TO RELATE WHO I AM IN A HEALTHY WAY

The main way we have to relate to one another is through communication. Words are necessary, yet words alone are not enough. Communication is much more than words. The tone of your voice and your body language really say more than your words. The expression of your body as you speak reveals more about you than any other part of communication. I am sure you have been accused of being disrespectful or angry with your parents by your tone of voice. Most of us have.

One of the drawbacks of communicating with words only is there are two ingredients missing. When you text message or email you cannot be sure what the other person is saying because you cannot see them or hear them. Pictures help but you still do not get the tone of voice. Healthy communication requires dialogue between two people. Each person has to be involved in telling and in listening.

WHAT DOES COMMUNICATION INVOLVE?

Communication that builds a relationship necessitates valuing the person you are putting into the relationship, otherwise you will be defensive with what is said to you and will begin to assume you know what the other person is thinking. Is anyone a good mind reader? No! Your part is to bring information about yourself to the relationship. You must also allow the other person to say who they are and accept who they are.

Communication also involves taking the time to discover what you have to give and how much you want to relate. I hope you have spent time deciding the valuable person you are in a relationship.

There are many kinds of relationships. We have social relationships which may only be a recognition of the other person. This is expressed when we address another person when we enter a room. It is called small talk. There is really nothing revealed about yourself except that you are present and you recognize the other person. This is often done with the question, "How are you?" Try greeting without a question. Most people find it difficult because it has become such a habit.

Functional relationships make it possible for you to live with those around you. This communication gives you an opportunity to let the other person know what you are doing or what you wish to contribute in working out life on a daily basis. Take a look at how many misunderstandings you have had with your parents because good communication was not used. Your mother may have asked you to meet her after school at a certain place and at a specific time. If you get only part of the message there will be a big mix-up and everyone will be unhappy.

There are many other kinds of communication but the emphasis of this book is personal relationships with God and others that we choose to be close to.

Relational communication requires preparation.
- You establish your valued identity.
- You have decided what you have to give to the relationship you want to build in the way of vulnerability, time and energy.

- You also have an idea of what qualities you are looking for in the other person.

WHAT ARE YOU LOOKING FOR?

Before you begin you need to know what you are looking for from the relationship with the other person. Is it to know them better? Do you have specifics that are important to you in a friendship? **What do you want?**

It is very important that you get accurate information about who they are from them. The information needs to be current. It is risky business to try to build off of old information or second hand information. This is very common in families. You can think you know what another person wants by past experience. Find out for today.

If you are looking to them to build you up you have too high of expectations of them. They will not always approve of what you think and do. If you are trying to connect in a meaningful way for both of you there is a good chance you will be successful.

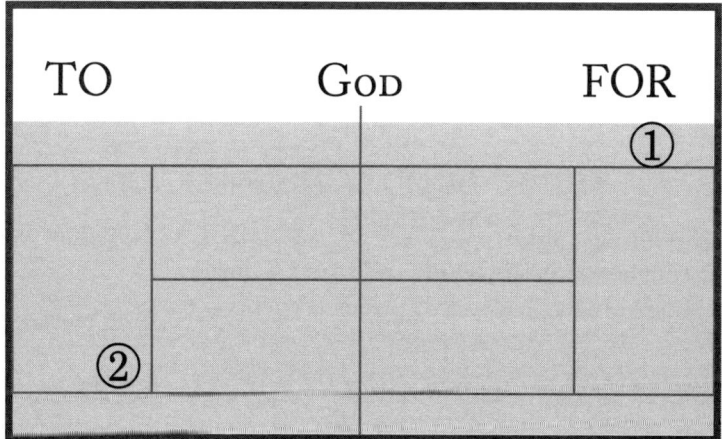

The example of how communication works will be drawn by the game of tennis.

With any game there are rules. In tennis the court is made up of two sides divided by a net. The net is for the purpose of defining what you are responsible FOR. Each player is only responsible FOR their side of the court. In this relational game the line judge is God. He has the rule book, the Bible, with the instructions of how each player is to be treated and what is out of bounds. Each player must play from their side of the court at all times. In communication, the object is to keep the ball (the subject) in play.

To leave your side of the court is to stop the game. The way you leave the court is when you try to tell the other person who they are or what they have to do to please you.

Let's do a typical conversation of a mother and daughter.

Daughter — "Mom, can I have some friends for a sleepover this weekend?"

Mom — "No."

Daughter — "Mom, you never listen so you always say, "No" before you hear me."

Mom — "Too much going on and I said, No."

The bickering can go on and on but this conversation cannot go anywhere? This is what I call lazy communication. There was no preparation made. We will work on this conversation after we have looked at the steps to good communication.

STEPS TO GOOD COMMUNICATION

Communication is very difficult whether it is being done by diplomats around the world or in your home.

There are five basis rules discussed here.

The first requirement in communicating.

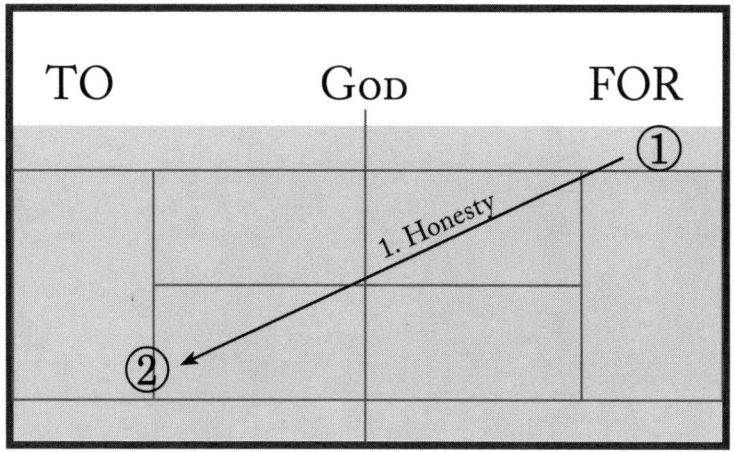

You must be honest with yourself and with the other person. Two of the ways you lie to yourself are letting others say who you are and believing others rather than what God says about your value. Honesty about yourself requires time and effort. You must not buy into others opinion of who you are or what you are supposed to do or be. Their opinion tells you about them not about you. Remember your belief system comes into play here. Define your own label of daughter or friend. What others have said to you and how they have treated you may cause you to place your value in their hands instead of discovering who you are today for yourself. Your concern needs to be what you are saying about yourself. If you tell the other person who they are you have left your side of the court so the game is halted.

Second requirement for healthy communication is listening to learn.

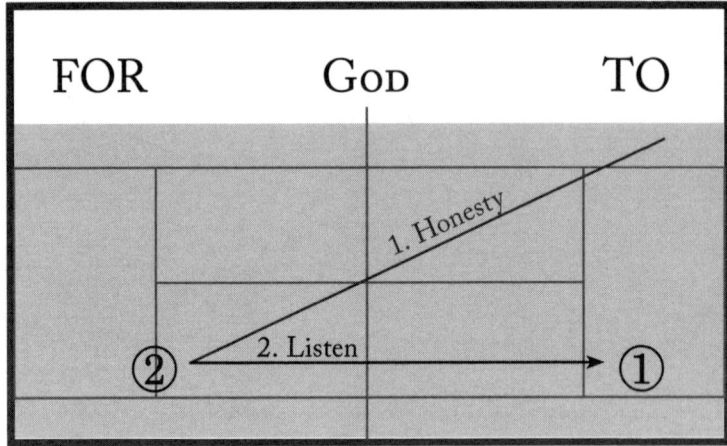

Listen to learn who the other person says they are. Very few people ever learn to listen to others to understand them. One of the number one complaints from teens is that they are not respected for who they are and they learn this because they are not listened to. One of the ways you show you value another person is to try to understand them. This cannot be done without listening to them. After you have spoken it is the other person's time to be heard. Listen so you can hear what they are saying about who they are and what they are thinking. When you can listen you have accurate information to work with in the relationship. Accurate information only comes from them. It cannot be assumed. Current information is also needed. Don't act on old information, it is history. Find out about today if you really want to know them. This is helpful in all relationships, even with God. Many times God does not get a chance to say who He is because someone has told you who they think He is. This is second hand information and often incorrect. Let His Word inform you who He is.

Number three is responding to what you have heard.

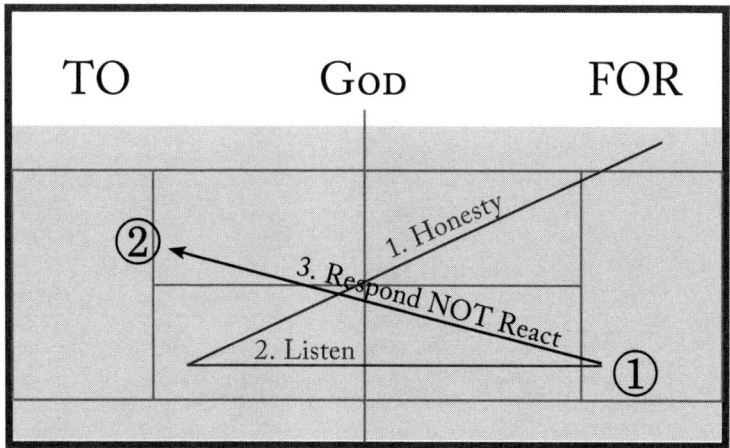

Listening is not complete until you have responded to the other person about what they have said. One of the ways you respect others is to respond to what they have said to you. Many times when you disagree your body language and your tone of voice will react to them. Reaction says you are not allowing them to be who they are and feel what they are feeling.

Number four—you get understanding when you are honest about yourself and listen to learn about the other person.

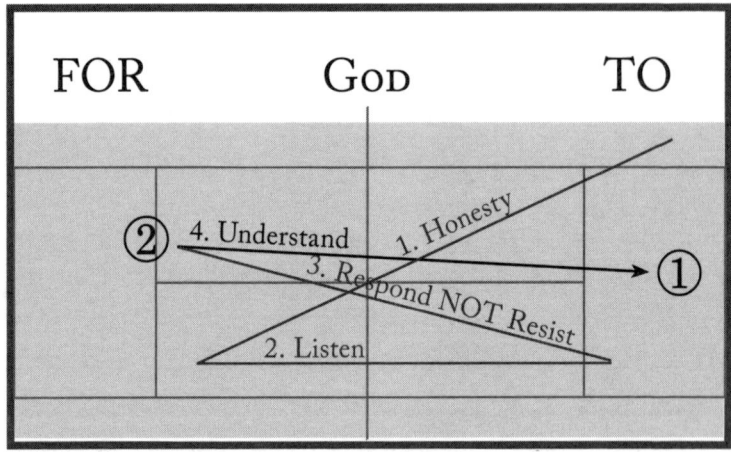

Understand so you can comprehend. Understanding comes through continued listening and responding to what they think or feel and where you are in your thinking and feelings. When you are communicating to understand it is not the time to correct or disapprove of the other person.

You do not need to try to convince them to think as you think. That would be a debate and not communication to build your relationship. One of the skills that is difficult to learn is honestly being who you are and letting the other person be who they are.

This becomes difficult when you try to express yourself to a parent and they start telling you what you should think or do. Don't give up. Listen to learn and then come back with what you think by asking them to please hear your thinking. It is very easy to give up on parents because you think you know what the final outcome of the discussion will be. Keep your mind on where you are and what it is you are trying to communicate to them.

Number five.

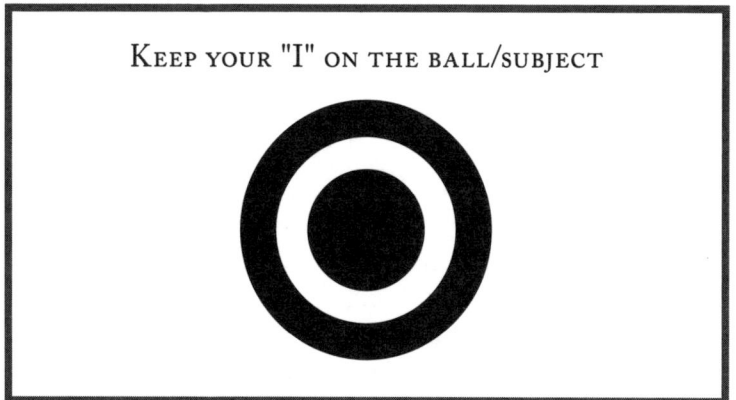

KEEP YOUR "I" ON THE BALL/SUBJECT

Attack the subject and not the person. Keep on the subject that you started on. Do not work on the other person or try to persuade them you are right. It is very important that you do not let them tell you what is right for you. This is your decision. They can only tell you what their thinking or feelings are about the subject.

The new information will help you make your final decision. Know that they want the best for you but may have a "listening" problem.

Let's work through the mother/daughter problem with our five steps.

Before the daughter begins to talk with her mother she needs to prepare herself by collecting information. This leaves no room for argument.

When does she want to have the sleepover?
Does she have a date in mind?
Why does she want to have the sleepover?
How many friends does she want to invite?
When does she want them to arrive?
Will transportation be needed to pick them up?

How long does she plan for them to stay?

What does she plan to do? Games? DVD? Movies? T.V.?

What kind of food does she want to serve? Pizza? Snacks? What?

What is she willing to do to prepare for their coming?

Now you are ready to approach your mother with your idea of a sleep over.

If you agree in principle you can work out the details by cooperation rather than opposition.

All of this is what you think, feel and are prepared to become involved in. If the answer is still, "No" then you must accept that is where your mother is at this time. She has a right to her opinion and feelings. If you have presented where you are that is all you can do.

It might be helpful for you to go over the rules for good communication by just sharing with a parent what you are learning. There is very little training for relational communication so they may not have had the opportunity you have had to discuss this. Let them see the excitement you have for learning how to communicate better.

11

WHERE DOES ANGER FIT?

THE EXPRESSION OF ANGER IS HEALTHY

When God started directing His People, Israel, out of bondage in Egypt to the Promised Land He gave them laws, the Ten Commandments. It was a completely different way of living than they had seen in Egypt. They had been in a country full of idols that needed to be appeased. They had not had an opportunity to worship the true and living God for over 400 years. They did not know how fair God was.

God always told His people where danger was and promised to protect them if they would follow Him as their God. When they followed they were protected. When they went off after other gods He did not protect them. When they repented and called on His name He rescued them and brought them back to Him.

God has always been for His people. When Jesus came into the world He came to explain who God is by interacting with the people. The Apostle Paul asked the church in Ephesus to contrast where they were before they came to Christ with who they are now in Christ. Look back and see the contrast of where they had been and where they are IN Christ. Because of all that is yours in Christ it is time to say "Yes" to God. The way to accomplish this is,

lay aside the old self, which is being corrupted in

accordance with the lust of deceit, and that you be renewed in the spirit of your mind, and put on the new self, which in the likeness of God has been created in righteousness and holiness of the truth. Therefore, laying aside falsehood, speak truth each one of you, with his neighbor, for we are members of one another. [62]

Deceit is the primary tool that misleads you. The way to overcome the deceit is by being renewed in the way you think about who God is, who you are, and accepting what He says about His love and concern for you. This new self is righteous and holy and truthful. Paul begins to talk about how to "put on the new self" with saying you are to stop lying and tell the truth to everyone.

How truthful are you?

Most people like to think they tell the truth most of the time. As we look at how we relate to others there is room to question how truthful we are in most situations. The temptation is to "please" and "not make waves" rather than speak the truth in love. Most everyone is trained to be "nice." Nice is fine if you are being honest and not just saying what you think the other person wants to hear.

But speaking the truth in love, we are to grow up in all aspects into Him who is the head, even Christ. [63] This passage is telling you to be truthful, genuine, honest.

Truth is absolutely necessary if you deal with your anger in a way that builds relationships.

Anger is expressed in many different ways but most often it is thought of as a person that is out of control.

What does anger look like to you?
- Is it a screaming Mimi?
- Is it a silent Susie?
- Is it a cry baby?

Another word for anger is displeasure. It doesn't give the

---

62 *Eph. 4:22–25 NASU*
63 *Eph. 4:15 NASU*

picture of a person that is out of control.

Self control is necessary in order to deal with anger. Most people prefer to "stuff" their feelings of anger rather than deal with them. This may be because you have never seen anger dealt with in a calm, rational way. Confrontation is simply good communication. When there is disagreement the issue needs to be confronted.

> ***BE ANGRY, AND YET DO NOT SIN;** do not let the sun go down on your anger, and do not give the devil an opportunity.* [64]

Anger is not wrong. When the word anger is mentioned most people think of someone who is raging and out of control. Look at the scripture and see what God is angry about. He is very displeased with anything that hurts you. He despises sin because of what it does to you.

Jesus was angry with the merchandisers selling their wares in the Temple.

> *Jesus entered the Temple and began to drive out the merchants and their customers. He knocked over the tables of the money changers and the stalls of those selling doves. He said, the Scriptures declare, My Temple will be called a place of prayer, but you have turned it into a den of thieves!* [65]

There are many reasons to be displeased in your world today. Life is not fair. It may be that your family is in conflict. It is possible that you have been hurt by someone close to you.

What would you say has caused you the most anger recently?

Is it parents who are not together, outside interference, mistreatment, abuse, lack of acceptance of who you are? Any one of these is painful.

---

64 *Eph. 4:26–27 NASU*
65 *Matt. 21:12–13 NLT*

How do you settle disagreements in your family?
- Are you allowed to express your anger?
- Can you be heard when you disagree with another member of your family?
- Are you willing to listen when a family member is upset with you?
- How much self-control do you use?

How do you express your anger?
- Do you retreat and stuff your feelings and implode? Is that being truthful?
- Are you called a "cry baby" when you are upset and cry?
- Are you told you are too sensitive when your feelings are hurt?
- Do you explode and attack others when you are angry?
- Do you make your anger about the other person and their treatment of you?

Unresolved anger is stored and carried with you. If denying you are angry is your pattern you need to consider it because it becomes a burden too heavy to carry after awhile. I am sure you have known an older person who was bitter and mean to others. That is what stored anger looks like when it is carried into the future instead of being resolved.

Learn to value yourself enough that you do not always have to be right. The root cause of anger is not being able to control others or your circumstances. Valuing yourself as God values you helps you to give others the respect of letting them be who they are without your correction.

The solution to your anger is doing your part. This is how scripture says to deal with anger. Anger is a given and the expression of it is healthy. It needs to be confronted at the time instead of waiting for it to resolve itself. There will not be an easier time than today. In other words the Bible says, do not store your anger for later because it gets out of proportion the longer you dwell in it. Not solving your differences with others will give the devil an opportunity to lie to you and help you to rationalize that it was all the other person's fault. This says they are in control of what you think and do.

If you are a thief, stop stealing. Begin using your hands for honest work, and then give generously to others in need. [66]

The Apostle Paul goes on with the emphasis of being responsible FOR yourself.

Dealing with anger and not stealing were new thoughts to the people of Ephesus. God's instructions were foreign to them. They had lived by what they wanted to do answering only to themselves. Paul told them not to steal but work so they would have something to share with those in need. Stealing had been the norm to them. He asked them to put off the stealing and put on the work so they would have something to give to those in need. The instruction today would be stop cheating and learn for yourself so that you will be prepared to be honest with others and do a good job in the work place.

Don't use foul or abusive language. Let everything you say be good and helpful, so that your words will be an encouragement to those who hear them.

And do not bring sorrow to God's Holy Spirit by the way you live, Remember, he is the one who has identified you as his own, guaranteeing that you will be saved on the day of redemption.

Get rid of all bitterness, rage, anger, harsh words, and slander, as well as all types of malicious behavior. Instead, be kind to each other, tenderhearted, forgiving one another just as God through Christ has forgiven you. [67]

---

66 *Eph. 4:28 NLT*
67 *Eph. 4:29-32 NLT*

Here are more new ideas for these new Christians to consider if they believed that God was for them. This was a new way for them to live. Wholesome talk, helpful talk, beneficial talk. This was a different guideline than the "World System" they lived in and the one you live in.

What would bring sorrow to God most? Would it be rejecting what He says to you about a healthy wholesome life? Be reminded that the Holy Spirit is grieved when He sees you doing harmful things to yourself or others. He wants unity and support among believers. One of the ways to make this happen would be to get rid of all bitterness, harsh words, rage, anger, slander and malicious behavior. They were being asked to live by a new standard.

Instead of all of the useless talk that hurts others the system according to God is to be kind, compassionate, and forgiving of one another. This can only happen if you see this is what Christ wants to give you. He is kind, compassionate and forgiving of you. **Do you accept His gift to you?** When you do, you have kindness, compassion and forgiveness to offer others.

You say, "This is well and good but what if the other person does not even want to talk with me?" You go back to understand what your part was in the disagreement. When you have figured that out and you are repentant it is time for you to ask them for forgiveness for your part. Saying you are sorry is not enough because it does not call for a response. It is just a statement of where you are. When you ask forgiveness with a repentant spirit you have done your part. You are asking for response on the part of the other person. It is up to them to either forgive you or hold you accountable to them until they are willing to let it go. It becomes their burden to carry until they are willing to forgive you.

The purpose of forgiveness is to restore a relationship. It is necessary that both parties have the desire to take responsibility for their part of the disagreement. Consider this. Even though Jesus paid the penalty for everyone's sins, *For God was in Christ, reconciling the world to himself, no longer counting people's sins against them. This the wonderful message he has given us to tell others.*[68] His **part**, you are still required to admit you have sinned and repent and ask forgiveness for rejecting Him. That is **your part**.

If the other person has not asked your forgiveness they must answer to God.

> *Do not take revenge, my friends, but leave room for God's wrath, for it is written: "It is mine to avenge; I will repay," says the Lord. On the contrary: If your enemy is hungry, feed him; if he is thirsty, give him something to drink. In doing this, you will heap burning coals on his head. Do not be overcome by evil, but overcome evil with good.* [69]

God knows all parts of what is going on and He will deal justly with each person. Your part is to check your attitude and see if you would be willing to forgive them if they asked. There is enough evil in the world. God does not want you adding to it but to be "light" as He is "light." To "get even" with others means you hurt yourself the most. Is that why the scripture says to let God be the judge and render justice when it is appropriate?

HURTS THAT ARE YOURS TO RESOLVE

There are times when you are displeased and harbor ill will toward another because of what they have done, said, or implied. When there has been no interaction between the two of you it is yours to resolve with God. Maybe your friend Jane has tried to tell you what you should be doing about your relationship with another friend, Kari, and you have been

---

68 *2 Cor. 5:19 NLT*
69 *Rom. 12:19–21 NIV*

insulted by her comments. The easy thing to do is try to justify your actions or to want to tell her where she is failing miserably in your opinion. It is more productive to talk to God about it and work it out with Him. Since you can talk to Him about anything this is a good time to tell Him exactly how you are feeling and what you think should be done. He hears you and loves you. He will help you to work through this and give you ideas. He may even remind you that He loves her as much as He loves you. He wants to help you find answers to your life that will build you up not tear you down.

The more anger you resolve as you go through your life, the more peaceful your life will be.

REMEMBER—the main cause of anger is your inability to control others or the circumstances around you.

12

LOVE, WHAT IS IT?

HOW TO RECEIVE LOVE

What says love to you?

This is very interesting because love is hard to define. We use the same four letter word to say we love a person, an animal, an article of clothing, a flavor of ice cream and on and on.

Love is needed by everyone in order to be healthy. Love is one of the expressions that build you up and helps you to know you are a valuable person. You can have your physical needs met but still not feel loved.

How does love work?

Is love a feeling or is it a fact?

There are a number of kinds of love but we will discuss three different kinds of love.

The first is Physical Attraction which is not mentioned in the New Testament. This is the emotional excitement when girl meets boy. This is often what is referred to when someone says, "We just fell in love." This is a feeling of excitement that can easily be "fallen out of" when the excitement wears off. It is a physical emotion. Infatuation is a thoughtless passion, a great, often temporary and irrational passion for someone or something. It may even be called an obsession. This can become a fixation so you can think of nothing else. This is not relational in any way. This is totally dependent on how the other person behaves toward you.

The "World System" says love is anything you do for me that makes me feel special. It is described when the Apostle John says,

> *Do not love the world nor the things in the world. If anyone loves the world, the love of the Father is not in him. For all that is in the world, the lust of the flesh and the lust of the eyes and the boastful pride of life, is not from the Father, but is from the world. The world is passing away, and also its lusts; but the one who does the will of God lives forever.* [70]

Look at how easy it is to be deceived by thinking how good the person looks, or I could have so much more of the world goods or popularity if I pleased them. Think about what happened to Eve in the Garden of Eden following the "looks good" logic. Be reminded that all of this is passing away or in other words will not fulfill the promises it makes. The "will" of God is that you relate to Him in Christ. He wants only the best for you. Eternal life is what last forever.

Another kind of love is between friends. A friend is someone you have affection for, a personal attachment. It is called *phileo*. This kind of love grows in friendships. You learn to care for one another and encourage one another to be their very best.

God's kind of love is *agapao*. LOVE.

Love is the highest expression of God and His relation to mankind, so it must be the highest expression of man's relation to his Maker and to his fellow-man.

This is the way God loves you and asks that you love others.

How do I understand it for myself?

It is important that you understand how much God loves you and how He has expressed His love for you. Take a look at the following scripture to get a real definition of love toward you and how you can express it to others.

---

[70] *1 John 2:15–17 NASU*

Dear friends, let us continue to love one another, for love comes from God. Anyone who loves is born of God and knows God. But anyone who does not love does not know God—for God is love.

God showed how much he loved us by sending his only Son into the world so that we might have eternal life through him. This is real love. It is not that we loved God, but that he loved us and sent his Son as a sacrifice to take away our sins.

Dear friends, since God loved us that much, we surely ought to love each other. No one has even seen God. But if we love each other, God lives in us, and his love has been brought to full expression through us. [71]

God is love and love only comes from God. It is for everyone but only a few ever accept it as it is given. You cannot love others without conditions if you do not accept God's love as it is given to you. God shows His love through those who have received it. One of the blessings that is yours is to believe what God says and trust Him enough to accept the love He offers to you. Look at the world around you. **How much love do you see being given to others without conditions? How much are you able to give?**

Let's let God define His love in actions. He has already said He is love. He proved His love by coming to die in your place for your sin of unbelief.

His love for you:

Is patient,

Is kind.

Does not envy, (jealous of or feelings against)

Does not boast, (haughty)

---

[71] 1 John 4:7–12 NLT

Is not proud.

Is not rude,

Is not self-seeking, (does not demand its own way)

Is not easily angered, (sharp—exasperated—irritable)

Keeps no record of wrongs.

Does not delight in evil but

Rejoices with the truth.

Always protects, (never gives up)

Always trusts, (never loses faith)

Always hopes,

Always perseveres. (endures through every circumstance) [72]

Have you ever thought of God loving you like this? He defined what real love is and what it looks like in everyday life.

Take each one of these characteristics of love and look at how you can understand them in relationship to God and you.

Can you be patient with yourself in all kinds of situations? God is.

What does kindness look like? Are you kind to yourself? God is.

The opposite of envy is having confidence in yourself that you are valuable because He says you are, in other words, believe God.

Learn to love yourself and not be comparing with others to see if you are okay. Receive your value from God.

Care for your own needs instead of expecting others to care for them.

Do not be arrogant thinking, I can do it by myself. Let God love you.

---

[72] *1 Cor. 13: 4–7 NIV*

Be polite to yourself.

Be considerate and give yourself room to be less than perfect.

Be pleasant and enjoy yourself.

Let God communicate who He is to you and tell Him who you are today.

Go free because God has forgiven you when you asked.

Do not be critical of yourself.

Accept life as it is—not asking for preferential treatment.

Be your own best friend.

Believe in yourself.

Major on what you do right not what you do wrong.

Accept the value God places on you.

Understand His love is beyond measure and endless.

When you have accepted God's unconditional love, you are ready to give to others. I like this statement made by Galileo Galilei, "All truths are easy to understand once they are discovered; the point is to discover them." This has always been true. **Are you ready to discover how much God loves you?**

13

WHY DATE?

WHAT DATING HAS TO DO WITH LOVE

It is a general assumption in our society that everyone is sexually active. This is not true. However, if you have been sexually active I want to state up front that this behavior does not have to be continued. You may have been caught up in the moment and compromised yourself but it does not mean you have to keep on that course.

Or if you have become sexually active seeking approval, love, significance, acceptance or just using a person you have a choice to stop, think, and decide what is best for you. Everyday is fresh and new for you to make up your own mind what you choose for your life.

Think about these questions:

To you what is the purpose of dating?

Is it to build your self-esteem?

Does it say something about how attractive you are?

Is it for the reason of being connected with someone so you feel you are accepted?

Are you spending the time you are together getting acquainted with each other?

Are you interested in a friendship with this person?

Why are you dating this particular person?

Does he have interests in common with you?

What kind of a reputation does he have?

Is he respectful of you in all areas?

Are you using all of your time with one person?

Is dating exclusive to you? When?

Do you think sexual abstinence before marriage is possible for you?

These are a few of the questions you need to be asking yourself if you are spending significant time with a guy.

These questions also need to be asked if you are just hanging out. The people you spend your time with have an enormous influence on you. Temptations come through people so it is important you spend your time with people who respect you and add something to your life. It is never a good idea to try to rescue someone in a dating situation. They need more help than you are capable of giving. If they are not okay to you the way they are it would be wise to move on.

At what age were you beginning to be pressured to say who your boyfriend was? Kindergarten? First Grade? There was more pressure put on you at an early age than you may realize. A subtle message is probably being given to you that if you do not have a male interested in you there must be something wrong with you. How many movies, DVD's, magazines, and TV programs are obsessed with finding the right person? The expectation of finding "Prince Charming" is placed on every young girl. Someone is supposed to come to your rescue and make everything wonderful in your life. Many girls jump too quickly into a relationship for fear they will miss their opportunity to be with the "right" person. Others feel it is God's responsibility to find the right person for them.

What is our culture saying to you about who you are in relationship to dating?

Do you believe the messages around you more than you believe God?

The primary purpose of dating at your age is to get acquainted with the males around you. I believe that a prerequisite to dating is to think ahead of time who you want to be and what you want for your life. Establish where your true value comes from and reject any other sources you may want to follow to fulfill your needs for worth, love and happiness.

Strive to become a person who has something to give to others rather than constantly looking for others to meet your needs. Go out and have fun with lots of different people and explore your interests and try new things. Think ahead if you want to be seriously committed to one person during your young teenage years. Foremost, don't believe the lie that says you must have a boyfriend or something is wrong with you. If a boyfriend is that important to you ask yourself if he has become god to you? He is if you are letting him control your value.

Dating is a time of getting acquainted with boys.

Look closely to see if they are respectful of those around them.

Is this person contributing to your life or are they constantly causing you to struggle with your own belief system?

What do you have in common?

Do you have the same desire to learn and grow?

Is your time well spent with him?

What is his reputation with your peers? Many times your peers have had experiences with him that would give you excellent information.

How does he relate to adults and their instruction?

Is he in trouble at school?

Where is your consideration of God in all of this? God does

not choose for you but He has a lot to say about what brings richness to your life.

Be alert at the beginning of your acquaintance with a guy. It is easy to let your emotions cloud your perception of him. The fact that a person is fun to be with is not the only criteria to look at.

True friendship with a male does not include personal contact. Once you start touching, your emotions begin to take over and it is difficult to see "red flags" waving before your eyes. Many young women have been trapped in a wrong relationship by emotional attachment. Are you the one always saying "No" with the physical progression?

What if you get stuck in a relationship that is taking you in a wrong direction? This is a very hard place to be in. There is not an easy way to break the relationship off. It's one of the most important choices you'll ever make—**Do I distance myself from my friend in order to be true to myself and to God? Or do I keep on going along and being controlled by what he wants?** It's a choice and it's a hard one. There could be strong opposition in your direction for a while. This takes a courageous stance on your part. Friendships should be building you up not tearing you down.

How many friends have you lost by dating exclusively too soon? If you do not have time for other friends when you are dating you are isolating yourself too much. It is hard to see a person for who they really are outside of being in group settings. Group activities are necessary for your own growth and to see how others act.

When you decide you are ready for an exclusive relationship be sure both of you are ready for commitment. It means that you will be committed to each other alone. You are off limits to anyone else, and so is he. This is an open-ended commitment, is it not? I mean, you're not saying yes to marriage…only to dating him alone for now...until...it doesn't work out...or marriage...whichever comes first. You are committing yourself to one guy!

The expectations of commitment have different levels of meaning to different people. What is usually the case is one person is "more committed" than the other. One doesn't measure up to the other's expectations. Each has different needs or reasons for being in the relationship. One might want another "notch on his belt." One might be very needy for attention or affection. One might want to fit in with the crowd. **Would you rather date just anyone, rather than no one?**

Where does commitment lead? One of the first elements is the beginning of the physical relationship. Touching starts. Shoulders, hands, then lips. The more comfortable you become with each other, the easier progression takes place. The Bible teaches clearly that sexual intimacy is reserved only for marriage between a man and a woman. You know that sexual feelings are normal and strong. So, you have come to a moral and personal decision.

If you have not thought through ahead of time what your convictions are in this area things will just "happen" and few, if any, will have self-control enough to stop. The only thing that will stop the physical intimacy, besides a natural disaster, is someone in the relationship having the convictions to control the sexual progression. Sex is more of a physical, visual, and immediate appeal for boys and more of an emotional response for a girl. If you go into this area naively, without understanding what is happening, it is like jumping out of a plane not knowing you need a parachute.

God's ideal plan is for the protection of your emotional and physical health. When you make a strong personal decision early in your life you honor God. This shows you respect yourself and your dating partners enough to leave that area to your future spouse untouched and unharmed. Take that stance now? The best way to follow through with that commitment is to know your value in Christ and what He desires for you. Anything else just doesn't compare!

Look at the scenario when you abuse the plan God has for your sexual relationship in marriage. Many teens treat sex like a recreational activity, using others for their pleasure without any thought of the emotional bonding that occurs.

Did you forget who thought up the idea of SEX? When God created man and woman in His image He made them to bond and become one flesh in marriage. This is such a special relationship that it is reserved only for marriage. The only other oneness relationships are you and Christ and Christ and God. It is sacred because you have the example of Christ and God as One. A married couple becomes a unit with a male part and a female part. Each one brings their self to the relationship.

Sex outside of marriage is using the other person for your own gain. It may seem like a connection that counts but it is not. Emotional injury occurs every time someone is sexually used. What good is a string of broken relationships by the time you're an adult? It only creates hurdles that have to be overcome as an adult. A teen lifestyle of sexual progression leads to a heart full of pain, guilt, shame, and self loathing, contrary to Hollywood's message.

Casual sexual play is extremely damaging, not only because of the possibility of pregnancy or disease, but also because of what it leaves behind—guilt, emotional suffering, resentment, shame. It devalues or makes cheap what God has designed as very intimate and special.

Do you know why God says what He does about sex outside of marriage?

The Apostle Paul writing to the new believers in Corinth said, *You may say, "I am allowed to do anything." But I reply,*

"Not everything is good for you." And even though "I am allowed to do anything," I must not become a slave to anything.[73]

This is a good time to ask yourself who is my Master? It can be your own desires or it can be trying to please another so you will be accepted. This is a very serious question.

You may say,"Food is for the stomach, and the stomach is for food." This is true, though someday God will do away with both of them. But our bodies were not made for sexual immorality. They were made for the Lord, and the Lord cares about our bodies.[74]

How do you determine what immorality is? Morals are only judged by what God says. One of the reasons for our permissive society is that everyone says what is right or wrong according to their own desires. Christ is concerned about your body and it being protected. How does He protect it? He protects it by you following what He says to you in His Word.

And God will raise our bodies from the dead by his marvelous power, just as he raised our Lord from the dead. Don't you realize that your bodies are actually parts of Christ? Should a man take his body, which belongs to Christ, and join it to a prostitute, he becomes one body with her? For the Scriptures say, "The two are united into one." But the person who is joined to the Lord becomes one spirit with him.[75]

God's word paints a graphic picture here of what is happening when you are sexually active outside of marriage. He calls it prostitution. You may say how can this be prostitution? A prostitute sells her body to get something she wants.

What is it you want?

Is it fitting in and being accepted?

Is it for attention so you will feel significant?

---

73 *1 Cor. 6:12 NLT*   75 *1 Cor. 6:14–17 NLT*
74 *1 Cor. 6:13 NLT*

Is it to say you are worth something to someone?
Is it to feel adult and in control?
Is it to get even with a guy who has ditched you?
It may be if you have done it once what difference does it make?

He follows the definition with a strong statement, "Never!" Not what He wants for you.

You leave a part of who you are with any sexual encounter because you have become one with that person. **Do you see why there is such an injury to you physically, emotionally, and spiritually?** This is a very hurtful thing to Christ because of what it is doing to you.

But the person who is joined to the Lord is one spirit with Him. [76] Paul clearly states that Christians are to have no part in sexual immorality, even if it is acceptable and popular in our culture.

Here is the power to overcome the temptation of the moment. Remember who you are and who you belong to. Christ will give you the strength to walk away from the temptation when you make the choice to go.

Flee immorality.

The warning has been made by God but it is up to you to get out of there. Do not surrender. Remember there is a way of escape with every temptation. You do not have to be overcome. It is a choice.

> *Run away from sexual sin! No other sin so clearly affects the body as this one does. For sexual immorality is a <u>sin against your own body</u>. Or don't you know that your body is the temple of the Holy Spirit, who lives in you and was given to you by God? You do not belong to yourself, for God bought you with a high price. So you must honor God with your body.* [77]

---

76 *1 Cor. 6:17*
77 *2 Cor. 6:18–20 NLT*

Every other sin that a person commits is outside the body, but the immoral person sins against his own body.
How do you sin against your own body?
Where is your self-respect?
Do you think this will have no effect on you and your future?
Are you saying you really do not believe God, He is just a killjoy?
Have you any respect for the other person?
What does sexual activity looks like outside of marriage. I want to use an ant colony as an example. Ants are pesky little insects and it is normal to want to get rid of them when they start to invade your home. To eradicate the ant you set up bait to attract them. The bait is poison to them but they eat it and carry some of it back to their colony. When the other ants eat the poison they all die. More ants go out in search of food and become attracted to the poison and continue to go through the same process until all of the bait is gone.

Girls whose desire is to be attractive to the male to gain their own sense of acceptance and significance are like the ant bait. They are ready to poison a young man's life while they are being diminished. The point is that both are being destroyed. The ant is destroying itself to satisfy his appetite. The attractive trap is losing herself little by little. She is being robbed or is giving away something that cannot be recovered.

TRUTH OR CONSEQUENCES?

It is difficult to even know what the consequences will be of promiscuous behavior. Sometimes the truth is garbled when it comes from peers, the media, or even from your own background. A good guide for you is if it has to be done in secret it will bring guilt and shame later. **Ask yourself, "What am I trying to buy by giving myself as the price?"**
Do you know what lies look like and sound like?

- You can be promiscuous and use men and walk away unscathed.
- You live in today's world and the only thing you will receive is rejection if you do not go along.
    My question is by whom? Those that want to steal from you something very precious—your self-respect.
- Don't be old fashioned. That was for another generation.
- You are worthless and out of date.
    By whose standard? Where does your value come from?
- Abstinence is impossible. You will be a prude.
    What does sex before marriage say about you? How is that your identity?

If you have already been sexually active you can begin today to change the course of your life and say, "No." It takes determination, energy, and self-control to accomplish the turn around. God promises to give you the strength when you make the commitment to yourself and to Him.

Remember God is for you He is not your enemy. The "World System" is your enemy and is trying to steal your future from you.

It is difficult for you to discern between the truth and lies about sexual relationships before marriage. Truth is what God says and He is trying to protect you. He is preparing you for a full and meaningful life whether married or unmarried. This time of dating is an excellent time to see how truthful the other person is and how honest you are willing to be with yourself.

> *Or do you not know that your body is a temple of the Holy Spirit who is in you, whom you have from God, and that you are not your own?*
>
> *For you have been bought with a price: therefore glorify God in your body.* [78]

Who do you belong to? Your decision to walk with Christ

---

[78] 1 Cor. 6:19-20 ??

is a place of worship. You are honoring Christ when you recognize that He dwells in you and it trying to lead you to abundant life. You bring glory to His name when you believe Him enough to overcome the temptation of buying into the "World System" that is trying to destroy you.

The teenage years should be years of finding who you are and what you like; what your talents and interests are. It could be a time of adventure, meeting people, trying new things you are interested in. How wonderful to think you could be 22 years old and look back at good times, good friends, and good things you have done, with much more to come! Look at the two different scenarios of your teenage years.

1) A long (or short) list of broken relationships and friendships.
Years of being robbed.
A low self worth that is based on boys' attention.
A pattern of needing boy's attention, no matter if he is mature, kind, responsible, or even a Christian.

Or the second scenario,
2) Freedom to be who you are.
Active in school and sports or clubs, church, family, and community.
Pure sexual life to bring to a marriage.
No regrets, shame or guilt.
Good friendships with both girls and guys.
Freedom to make life choices like college, jobs, trips.

Walk, don't run. Give yourself time to learn what it is you want to do with your life. Teens are rarely ready at this early age for one hundred percent commitment to a guy. Don't expect something that someone else is not ready to give at this young age. Be content knowing where your real value comes from. When you catch yourself in your mind saying "no guys like me because…" or "I'm so ugly, fat, stupid…", stop yourself and recognize what you are doing to yourself. Replace those words with the truth. "I am loved and valued." "I have a lot to give. I am confident. I respect myself."

Be careful that you're not buying into the popular philosophy that all things "hot and sexy"; all things fun; all things cool are the most important things to obtain in this world. Step back and realize where this message comes from. Marketers basically want your money, right? And they sell whatever is attractive and whatever will make you "cool" with your peers. You are their #1 market. It all goes back to feeding your need for acceptance.

What is your focus? Is it to be accepted by what others define as cool, or is it to be true to what you really want for your life and what God wants to help you with?

14

YOUR FUTURE

WHAT ARE YOUR DREAMS FOR THE FUTURE?

After you have dreamed awhile it is time for a few questions. **Who are your models to reach your dreams?** It is easy to dream of "happy ever after" without looking at how this happens. Some ideas to consider.
- Be your own person. Let God say what is available to you.
- Learn to accept one thing at a time. Dwell on who you are to God for one month and see if your thinking about yourself changes.
- Learn to speak for yourself. Your opinions and ideas are as good as anyone else. They contribute who you are.
- Learn to receive the love God wants to give you. You can only truly love another when you accept how God loves you. *We love, because He first loved us.*[79] These are just words unless they become the way you think about yourself.
- Observe how you express your anger. When dating be aware of how the guy pressures you to change with his anger.

Purpose in life is determined by what you decide is valuable enough to invest your time in. Every life can find purpose. Purpose means you have a direct intention of doing something with your life. It determines which direction you choose to take. You can decide to live out your life as a believer in Christ or ramble along in your own way hoping life will be good to you. Being a good influence is a great purpose for your life.

If you have chosen Christ you have help in deciding the direction you take. Look at what you have to work with. **Do you remember the parable of the talents in scripture?** This is a parable. A parable is an illustration that has a central meaning. Read this and see what you think He is saying to get the believers to understand about His return. Don't take it apart. Just read it and see what the message is regarding His return.

> *It's also like a man going off on an extended trip. He called his servants together and delegated responsibilities. To one he gave five thousand dollars, to another two thousand, to a third on thousand, depending on their abilities. Then he left. Right off, the first servant went to work and doubled his master's investment. The second did the same. But the man with the single thousand dug a hole and carefully buried his master's money.*
>
> *After a long absence, the master of those three servants came back and settled up with them. The one given five thousand dollars showed him how he had doubled his investment. His master commended him: 'Good work! You did your job well. From now on be my partner.'*
>
> *The servant with the two thousand showed how he also had doubled his master's investment. His master commended him: 'Good work! You did your job well. From now on be my partner.'*
>
> *The servant given one thousand said, 'Master, I know you have high standards and have careless ways, that you demand the best and make no allowances for error. I was afraid I might disappoint you, so I found a good hiding*

place and secured your money. Here it is, safe and sound down to the last cent.'

The master was furious. That's a terrible way to live! It's criminal to live cautiously like that! If you knew I was after the best, why did you do less than the least? The least you could have done would have been to invest the sum with the bankers, where at least I would have gotten a little interest.

Take the thousand and give it to the one who risked the most. And get rid of this "play-it safe" who won't go out on a limb. Throw him out into utter darkness. [80]

Do you hear Jesus saying to believe who He is, believe what He says and use what He has given you to relate personally to Him? He is for you. He is interested in you. He values you just the way you are today. As you relate to Him you will find relating to others much easier.

The scripture continues to say that the emphasis is on helping one another by relating as believers to one another. How is this done? Since Christ established the Church to be the family of God there is much said about how we are to relate to one another.

How do you do this at home with your family?
With Parents?
With siblings?
What do your relationships look like with your friends? Your peers at school?
Invest yourself totally. Your influence is much more important than the impression you are trying to make. Your influence is your most powerful statement of who you are. Rather than being a person who goes along with the crowd be a person of influence who does what she knows to be right.

---

80 Matt. 25:14–30 The Message

A RELATIONSHIP CAN ONLY EXIST WHEN TWO PEOPLE ARE WILLING TO CONNECT WITH ONE ANOTHER. Be responsible FOR yourself.

Connection happens when there is:

VALUED IDENTITY where approval from the other is not necessary to be okay but what God says about your value to Him is most important.

RESPECT to be able to listen to the other person's opinion without criticism—caring to understand them

FRIENDSHIP caring for the other person and giving room to grow—listening to a different opinion to learn who they are.

SAFE AREA—knowing the other person is committed to building the relationship and cares as you do.

HONESTY—no withholding of information about self that pertains to the relationship. Willing to be open about what you feel and think about real matters

TRUST—exercised on the basis of record. Trust is gained as you see the trustworthiness of the other exhibited as they continue to relate. Trust is earned.

> *My prayer is I ask the God of our Master, Jesus Christ, the God of glory—to make you intelligent and discerning in knowing him personally, your eyes focused and clear, so that you can see exactly what it is he is calling you to do, grasp the immensity of this glorious way of life he has for Christians, oh, the utter extravagance of his work in us who trust him—endless energy, boundless strength!* [81]

---

81 Eph. 1:17–18 The Message

Woman—Aware and Choosing also has a ten-week course available for teaching the basic principles with tools for building healthy relationships.

A training course is available to potential teachers of this material.

For further information:

MinMar Press,
P.O. Box 1658
Brea, CA 92822
Minmarprs@aol.com
www. Bettycoblelawther.net